ONE EVENT THAT CHANGED HISTORY OF EARTH

SON OF MAN

Becomes

SON OF GOD

TRINITY ROYAL

Son of Man becomes Son of GOD

One Event that Changed History of Earth

Trinity Royal

result of the use of the information contained within this document, including, but not limited to, errors, omissions, or inaccuracies

Library of Congress Control Number: 2022919526

Contents

Free books to our readers

War in Heaven came to Earth. Satan Rebellion:

https://dl.bookfunnel.com/ea12ys3dmk

Your Life in Heaven:

https://dl.bookfunnel.com/vg451qpuzs

INTRODUCTION

E very human being, young and old, male or female, from any part of the world, has to deal with challenges in their life. We all also have to make choices and, in many cases, resist temptation. Sometimes we have to choose between an action pleasurable in the short-term and another more profitable in the long-term, or between actions that could hurt others but benefit us personally, or those which require sacrifice on our part but benefit society as a whole.

The most significant and best-remembered stories often involve choices like these, and these themes also show up in the great religions of the world, capturing universal truths as they do.

The Abrahamic religions are no exception. Both the Old and New Testaments are filled with examples of men and women who have had to choose between serving themselves or God, between sacrificing for the right thing or doing the wrong thing for short-term profit. This book is about one such important choice Jesus Christ made in the New Testament, and will examine the reasons He made that choice, the effects it had on the subsequent course of human history, and what would have happened if He had failed and made a different choice instead.

You may have heard of the temptation of Christ in the wilderness, but have you ever considered what would have happened if Christ had failed?
It was one of the greatest battles in the history of humanity and the planet Earth itself. The fate of Earth, and many worlds beyond it, hinged upon its outcome. Yet it was not fought with swords and shields, nor bullets and tanks. One side did not even take up arms. It was not a physical struggle. And most of all, absolutely no one except its participants witnessed its progress and ultimate outcome, even though all of history would have been radically different if the other side had won.

This famous spiritual duel is recounted in three of the gospels of the Bible and tells of Christ's victory over the devil during a time of temptation by the latter. Much ink has been spilled throughout the years around this event, including the hypothetical question as to whether Christ could have actually given into temptation. While this topic has been broadly discussed, most scholars have omitted the hypothetical consequences as to what would have happened if Christ had failed against His adversary during this act of warfare. This book wishes to explore this lesser-traveled theological path, answering some pertinent questions that arise when considering this suppositional altered course of events.

For such a topic to be properly addressed, it becomes crucial to consider the persons involved in the event, the event itself, and all the possible outcomes that could have arisen, while looking at the actual outcome, and the implications thereof. For this reason, some time will be spent looking at the devil, considering his fall from grace and the extent of his power on earth. Next, the person Jesus Christ will be examined with respect to His nature, life, ministry, purpose, and relationship with the Father. It is of course pivotal to zoom in on the temptation itself, making sense of what actually transpired in the wilderness. This will be followed by three questions, namely whether Christ could have given to Satan's temptations, what would have happened if He did, and what it means for us today that He did not.

Specifically, this book focuses on the Devil's temptation of Jesus on the great mountain,

Hermon. There, the forces of darkness offered Christ lordship over the entire world, but He made the right choice and stayed loyal to His Father, thus providing hope for salvation for all the rest of humanity on Earth—and, also the effect on the rest of the universe!

We will start at the bottom of things and gradually introduce the reader to all the theological and historical background he or she will need to truly understand the significance of Christ's victory over temptation. First, as a useful review for readers with a background in theology or Biblical studies, we'll go over how the Bible actually describes Christ's temptation, quoting from the books of Mark, Matthew, and Luke. We'll also go over its implications for the universe as a whole which many Christians may not be aware of. With the basics covered, the next chapters will explore the deeper background behind Christ's temptation, explaining what He was doing on Earth in the first place, and then why Lucifer rebelled against God and wanted to turn Jesus against the forces of Light.

We will then describe Christ's journey to Mount Hermon and preparation beforehand as well as why Satan chose that specific time as opposed to any other to attempt his subversion of the Savior.

Also, we will explore the ramifications of Christ's refusal to accept Satan's offer, and how this allowed the forces of Light a chance to triumph over those of the Dark. The final chapter will then explore a frightening counterfactual: What if Christ had accepted Satan's offer and gone over to the Darkness?

A number of questions and dilemmas will be visited as this topic is explored.

- What was Jesus's purpose in coming to Earth?
- What was the devil's goal in tempting the Son of Man?
- What was the extent of the power that each party possessed?
- Why did the devil choose the approach he did?
- Is there significance in the method of the victory Jesus employed?
- What were the consequences of Jesus's victory?
- What would have happened if the devil had successfully led the savior into his temptation?
- What does all this have to do with the reader today?

Let's witness His journey.

THE PREPARATION

When you see a successful person, you only see the tip of the iceberg. Their failures, hard work, long hours, and investment of effort, energy, and resources are often forgotten or overshadowed by their success. Spectacular achievement is always preceded by less spectacular preparation.

It is true in the world of sports – "Champions do not become champions when they win the events, but in the hours, weeks, months and years they spend preparing for it". The victorious performance itself is merely the demonstration of their championship character.

The importance of preparation is no less important when it comes to Christian living. Faithfulness. Spirituality. And Bible knowledge. Anything significant is preceded by intensive and thorough preparation (often behind the scenes). Things just don't happen. In fact, the quality of the preparation determines the quality and success of events.

- A delicious meal requires hours in the kitchen when no one else is around.
- An enjoyable musical performance requires hours of practice and preparation.
- A superb sports performance demands hours of training and preparation.
- A doctor spends years studying before he or she can take the tools and begins to operate (aren't you glad!).

- A significant ministry of high impact also requires the same intensity of preparation. God often takes his time.

The better the preparation, the more significant and lasting the impact. So in the spiritual. God prepares by His Spirit and we also must prepare. God sent John the Baptist to "prepare the way of the Lord". He was God's prophetic messenger sent before the coming of Messiah "to make ready a people prepared for the Lord (Luke 1:27)."
Every significant event for the purposes of God is preceded by a time of intense preparation.

Early Childhood

In Bible times, a Jewish boy became a man at 13. His father would train him to take on all the responsibilities of adulthood—social and spiritual. Joseph was a carpenter, and he likely trained Jesus in his trade. The Bible does not give many details about Jesus' childhood, but we know that as Jesus got older, He grew "in wisdom and stature, and in favor with God and with people" (Luke 2:52).

Communion with The Father

It is also important to note that Jesus communed directly with the Universal Father at a very young age, certainly before 20, but most likely in His teenage years. He learned the formal Jewish prayers from his parents, but He also caused them some consternation when, at times, it seemed like He was talking to God not reverently, but just as if He would talk to Joseph or Mary. Even after being spoken to, He would not change these habits but just insist He was having "little chats" with the Universal Father after saying the formal prayers Jews were expected to.

This is proof that Jesus truly was an incarnation of God the Father and thus had a direct line, so to speak, with Him. Though God listens to all our prayers, it can be difficult to realize that for most of us ordinary people. Jesus, however, was able to commune with Him directly, one-on-one, many times over the course of His youth, as well as His subsequent ministry as an adult.

Being about Father's Business

By the time Christ was a young adult, it was very hard to deny that He was very different from not only the people around Him but His own parents as well and that He had a special destiny. It was not yet apparent to the general population of Judea, but Jesus became aware of it by the end of His thirteenth year. At that time, an angel from the Universal Father descended and told Jesus everything about His special relationship with the Divine and His special mission on Earth. Jesus became aware of His divine status and His purpose. As He continued to grow up, He prepared more and more for his future of traveling and preaching, which would take him far away from His home and family. It would certainly be difficult, but it was a necessary step in the process of Bestowal and becoming the most worthy universal ruler possible—after all, His friends and family would not be around to help Him govern far-off solar systems and galaxies!

But, it was also very tough for His parents as well. Not long after the above events, He and His family had visited the great temple of Jerusalem together, but He had left them for several days, giving them a great scare. For one of the first times, they remonstrated Him, saying how worried they were, but He had been spending all that time preparing to deliver the Jewish people from Roman bondage. Jesus told His parents He loved them, and wouldn't worry them suddenly again. But He did imply that he would leave someday and did His best to prepare His family for that moment. As He said, "While I must do the will of my Father in heaven, I will also be obedient to my father on earth. I will await my hour".

This was what Jesus did: When the time was right, He took His leave from his beloved home and family, telling them "I have to be on my Father's business." But before He left, he made arrangements at home so that his parents are taken care of.

John Baptizes Jesus

John is trembling with emotion as he prepares to baptize Jesus in the Jordan. Thus did John baptize Jesus The men nearby heard a strange sound, and there appeared for a moment an apparition immediately over the head of Jesus, and they heard a voice saying, "This is my beloved Son in whom I am well pleased." A great change came over the countenance of Jesus, and coming up out of the water in silence he took leave of them, going toward the hills to the east.

After Christ's baptism by John, "at once the Spirit sent him out into the wilderness, and he was in the wilderness forty days, being tempted by Satan. He was with the wild animals, and angels attended him." (New International Version, Mark 1:12-13).

Matthew and Luke go into much more detail. After Christ's baptism, He left the Jordan River and was described as "full of the Holy Spirit," indicating that the forces of Light were watching over him and strengthened him spiritually Luke 4:1-2 says, "And Jesus being full of the Holy Ghost returned from Jordan, and was led by the Spirit into the wilderness, Being forty days tempted of the devil. And in those days he did eat nothing: and when they were ended, he afterward hungered."

No man saw Jesus again for forty days.

POWER OF LONELINESS – CHRIST'S STATE OF MIND BEFORE TEMPTATION

Given His affection for His family and friends, why would Jesus suddenly embrace solitude? What did He gain by separating himself utterly from the world He was sent to learn about and influence, especially right before embracing His mission?

Preparation is the key to success. So exactly how did Jesus prepare? Gospels specifically note that the trial lasted exactly forty days. This forty days is Christ's 'Dark Night of the Soul's journey.

Power of Solitude

The first thing you must understand is that seclusion specifically is not a unique occurrence. Most evolved spiritual beings have one thing in common: They have spent time in loneliness. Some famous hermits and anchorites have spent their entire adult lives in isolation, and even teachers and sages who returned to the world have done the same for short periods. Martin Luther King spent time alone in jail, where he wrote his famous letter; Ralph Waldo Emerson spent time by himself in the American wilderness for a while, where he was able to gain a firmer appreciation for the beauty of nature. This is a necessary step in the path toward spiritual growth, and even though these examples involve mere mortal human beings, divine entities like angels also gain these benefits from loneliness. In this section, we will go over what, exactly, the benefits entail and how they prepared Christ to triumph over temptation.

Given how stressful (mentally and physically) isolation can be, it is important to be prepared on both levels before spending time in loneliness. Christ did this by ensuring His family could live without Him before departing on His journey, but He also took steps on a personal level as well. He ate well and got plenty of rest, so He would be fit and have lots of energy for his sojourn on Mount Hermon, and He also spent a lot of time with His friends, family, and even little children in the places He visited, teaching them and spreading His knowledge where He could. Since He would be unable to see them for a while, getting as much interaction with them as possible before the trip fulfilled His needs for social interaction and camaraderie for a good while, so He wouldn't run out of his social energy reserves (so to speak) during His 40 day stay at Hermon (as this might have led to His mental state deteriorating rather than improving, obviously contrary to His objectives).

With that preparation complete, Christ was ready to enjoy these mental, spiritual, and physical benefits of loneliness:

Communion with God is strengthened

Out in the world of ordinary people, there are always many distractions that keep you away from God and higher spiritual matters. When you have to worry about your job or your car payments or taking care of your family, you have less time to worry about the state of your soul and what will happen to you in the afterlife. Even fun things can distract from these thoughts: it's hard to think of spiritual ascendance when you are playing sports or video games, or having fun with your family and friends. When you are completely alone, with only the beauty of the wilderness as your companion, all those distractions disappear. There is only you, God, and the beauty of the natural world He has created. Thus, your mind will be completely focused on the Universal Father, and it is much easier to achieve communion with Him. This is what Christ experienced.

Even though He already had a close relationship with the Father—far closer than most people, as evidenced by how He was able to chat casually with God in addition to praying formally—His isolation on Mount Hermon brought him closer to God, and thus made Him more enlightened about God's plans and desires than ever before.

Your character is formed

There is something important that a time of solitude brings out in us. The greatest communication that a man can ever have is communication with himself. Just like growth is worked out in plants within a specified time, as humans, the time of solitude for us will always be like that of the plant. Nobody is likely to see anything being produced in us because we are still or because we are not doing anything but the truth is that in our quietness, virtues are produced, a resonance with destiny is achieved, and an understanding of our spirit is enabled, we can perceive beyond the physical, we can decipher within every part of our life and find a hold in the center where every part is sustained from.

All the distractions in life can prevent you from understanding what's truly important, and thus, prevent you from realizing your best self and becoming as moral and virtuous as you could be. In other words, distractions can prevent your personal character from being properly formed, which means that loneliness can greatly aid in the formation of a strong, just moral character.

Communing with God for 40 days, and enduring the trials of hunger and a lack of social interaction, Christ grew more finely attuned to the pain of the unfortunate, the forgotten, and the impoverished—and He was already very empathetic towards such people in the first place! By separating Himself from them, and indeed, from everything in the world, He was able to reflect rationally and dispassionately on such things, and thus further deepen His conviction and ability to deal with them both as an individual man and as the Son of God.

Your soul transformation happens

As described earlier, human souls produce large amounts of spiritual energy when they ascend to higher levels. Isolation transforms your soul, the thinking and feeling part of a sapient being, into one capable of ascending in such a way.

Additionally, isolation means that the only thing on your mind is soul transformation, with no distractions to keep your eyes from that goal. This makes the process much more efficient, as it is almost impossible to get sidetracked and waste time on irrelevant things, or even lose sight of the truth and fall on the wrong path due to trickery or just a lack of discipline. A period of isolation can advance your soul massively in a short time, as well as greatly reduce the risk of failure.

Roots of service are planted

Loneliness encourages you to think of others before yourself and sets you on the path to living a virtuous life of service rather than self-aggrandizement. After all, one of the easiest ways to fall into materialism and selfishness is to constantly pursue social status and material gain. Even a virtuous soul, when receiving incessant praise from others due to performance at work, money, or even virtuous deeds, can grow haughty and uncaring. Such people say to themselves, "Looking good in the eyes of others is all that matters, rather than actually being good." However, when you're all alone, with no one else to praise or scorn you in the wilderness, you gain a much better sense of self and realize that external validation is meaningless because no one is around to constantly feed it to you. Thus, loneliness will teach you to focus only on virtue, which, as the old saying goes, is its own reward.

Loss of interest in material gains

When you separate yourself from people, you also separate yourself from the various material accouterments that accompany those people. Think of Christ's life before He went to Hermon: though He was not rich, He still had many possessions, ranging from the family home to carpentry equipment, to clothes, and so on. Totally alone on the mountain, however, all that would have seemed to be irrelevant. Thus, Christ cared even less than He already did about money, material possessions, and so on. A good vacation alone can effect the same change in you.

Possible detours in one's life

Loneliness can also open you up to new ways of living you might have been unaware of or never considered before. Sometimes, the pressures of the world, the day-to-day rat race, make us complacent and destroy our imaginations. We spend so much time chasing material goods or fame, or just worrying about our normal jobs in order to maintain the daily necessities, that we forget that things could have turned out differently. Sometimes we forget that, as spiritual beings with free will, there is an entire universe of possibilities out there for us. Spending time alone can re-open our eyes to these possibilities. When we have a chance to quietly reflect with no distractions or worries, we can understand what led us to where we currently stand, and where else we can go from that location, even if we never had the time or peace to really think about it before.

This was what happened with Jesus: Though He had already known He was destined to serve the Universal Father in a special way on Earth, a solitude on Mount Hermon allowed Him to better understand the myriad ways that were possible and eventually settle on the best course.

Introspection

Freed from worldly distractions, you can take a closer look at yourself to understand who you truly are. Surrounded by people all the time, they can mislead you (intentionally or unintentionally) as to what your true strengths and weaknesses are, through either unwarranted flattery or unhelpful harshness. By separating yourself from everyone and truly taking stock of yourself on your own, you can get an objective assessment of what you really need to change about yourself and what ought to stay the same, whereas the assessment produced by other people might be tainted by their prejudices or their desires for things other than virtue and spiritual ascendance.

Quality time with the Universal Father

Far away from even His friends and family, Jesus could focus on building an even closer personal relationship with Divinity. Though, of course, we will never know exactly what they talked about over the course of the forty days, it is safe to assume that Jesus could lay bare his concerns and worries to God even more forthrightly than He ever could praying at home or in the temple, where others might possibly have heard Him. Thus, the two could enjoy each other's company on a deeper level.

State of Earth Prior to First Coming - War in Heaven came to Earth

To really understand Christ's mission on this blue orb, we need to spend little time on why Christ decided to come to Earth.

While there are many reasons, the primary reason being - to pave the way for Human salvation and to teach and establish communion with God the Father with-in.

So what exactly happened on Earth and why is salvation lost or communion with God not known?

Who is Satan and what is his purpose on Earth? What does he want?

What does Satan have to do with Christ?

To be able to answer these questions, let us spend some time understanding the back-drop of planet Earth at the time of Christ's First Coming.

War in Heaven

All the major religions of the world including Christianity, Islam, Judaism, Hinduism, and Buddhism agree on one critical fact – there is Heaven and hell, God and His adversary, and Light and Dark, and both are opposites. The adversary is called by different names including Satan, Shaitan, Iblis, and Lucifer. All religions also agree both factions are powerful adversaries and that

Human beings are somehow part of this epic battle. Most of the details in all of the scriptural texts are either high-level or sketchy at best, there is no explanation. This is subject to different interpretations and confusion among theologians.

The Holy Bible when seen through the lens of history has more info comparatively than most other religious scriptures about the war in heaven but this also falls short. I have discussed in detail about the War in Heaven in my other books "Christ vs Satan – Final Battle for Earth has Begun, part of The Real Matrix" series. So will not be going into details; however, we will review this briefly.

To consider the devil's temptation of Christ, it is important we study briefly the dark forces at play behind the scenes. This will involve studying demonology, the identity of the devil, the fall of Lucifer, the development of the realm of darkness, the influence on Earth with the temptation of man, the extent of the devil's power then and now, and the purpose of the dark forces.

Misconceptions of the devil

A grand misconception about Satan is that he does not exist. What comes to your mind when you think of the devil? For many, they imagine him to be a small, red cartoon creature with a sneaky smile and a pitchfork. This may be one of the greatest misconceptions of the devil, merely a cartoon, and this is on an equal plane as other cartoons like Mickey Mouse and Bugs Bunny.

While it is wrong and unbiblical to think of our enemy as non-existent, it is also common to swing to the other side of the pendulum. Many have misconstructed the devil as being equal and opposed to God, as there are two cosmic powers, fighting to get the upper hand. This dualistic perspective is also unbiblical, as the scriptures never talk about Satan as being equal in power to God, but rather as being a created being that will one day be judged.

If Satan is not omnipotent, it must also be stated that he is not omnipresent. Another common misconception is that Satan can be in many places at one time. This is contrary to the scriptures, which show him as being a created being that wanders to and fro on earth (Job 1:7). Many people when they are facing a trial or hardship, attribute it to Satan. If this is true, it means that out of almost 8 billion people on earth, he is choosing to deal with, he can only be in one place at a time. That being said, the scriptures depict an army of demons that do his bidding, and so while a person may not be tempted directly by Satan, it could be that a demon is afflicting them on behalf of the devil and demonic forces.

These are simply a few of many misconceptions that exist regarding Satan in this age. By studying the scriptures on this topic, the falsehoods will be dispelled and replaced with the truth about the devil and demonology.

Identity of the devil

The devil has many titles in the Bible, such as Satan, Lucifer, Beelzebub, and others. The word Satan means "the adversary", the devil means "the accuser", and Lucifer which is used only two times in the Bible is translated as "star of the morning". The Bible uses these titles interchangeably, such as in Revelation 20:2 which says "He seized the dragon, the ancient serpent, who is the devil, or Satan, and bound him for a thousand years." Throughout the scriptures, it is clear that all of these titles refer to an entity that is opposed to God, and is identified by his attributes, "accuser", "adversary", and so on. In short, Satan or Lucifer is a fallen angel, but this necessitates further explanation.

Note: Lucifer and Satan or Devil names are used interchangeably in this book. Since the ideology is the same, the names are interchangeable.

The Devil as an Angel

God created angels at the time of creation (Gen 1, 2; Col 1). Colossians 1:16 states "For by Him all things were created, in heaven and on earth, visible and invisible, whether thrones or dominions or rulers or authorities – all things were created through Him and for Him". It is important to note that Satan then was created by God and is much inferior to God, and not a peer or equal, as some have erroneously supposed. The spiritual rules here are thought to refer to angelic beings. The scriptures testify that there are "myriad and myriad of angels" (Rev 5:11).

Amongst these heavenly hosts was Satan (Job 1; Ezek 28). He was created by God, along with the other angels, creatures, and humans, as being "very good" (Gen 1:31). This means that he was created as a spiritual being without a bodily form. Many hold that Satan was highly esteemed for his beauty and wisdom. This stems from

6

interpretations of passages such as Ezekiel 28:17a which says "Your heart was proud because of your beauty; you corrupted your wisdom for the sake of your splendor". Thus, we can venture to say that the devil was created as a sinless, beautiful angel and that at some point he fell from this state.

GOD vs Devil – The Fall of the Devil

God Created Lucifer as a unique being in that he was an Angel, the most beautiful angel of all created, and he had free will, and the ability to make his own decisions and act on them. The original Aramaic name Lucifer translates to Morning Star. Lucifer is mentioned in the Bible only two times but is said to have sat at God's side and worshiped him and loved him deeply. Lucifer was regarded as the wisest, greatest, and most beautiful angel in all of the creation. He is described as the most beautiful and brightest angel in existence and regarded as the perfection of beauty and wisdom. His beauty exceeded all other angels in heaven to the point where a mere glance would make anyone go mad from sheer beauty and power. He is noted to have six colossal whitish gold wings, that almost looked made of light. According to the old testament, when

Lucifer was in heaven his clothing was adorned with many precious stones all beautifully crafted for him and set in the finest gold.

Due to Lucifer being the favored creation, God would reveal to him, His plans for the creation. The more God told Lucifer His plans, the more problems Lucifer began to see in God's plan. His thoughts began to stray from what his Father desired. Eventually, it led to a series of heated arguments between God and Lucifer. Lucifer's

paranoia made him see God as a tyrannical ruler and declared that he had a better plan for the universe and that he would exalt his throne above God. Lucifer finally launched his "Declaration of Liberty".

"I will ascent into heaven, I will exalt my throne above the stars of God; I will also sit on the mount of the congregation on the farthest sides of the north; I will also ascend the heights of the clouds, I will be like the Most High." – Isaiah 14:13-14

He proposed a new Creation concept. Lucifer sincerely believed that with his new creation, he could enhance and fasten spiritual growth compared to the current process of step-by-step evolution under God's rule. Lucifer wanted to be the creator of souls, he thought that by using laboratory methods, machine intelligence, and his creative abilities, he is able to give a portion of himself to create new souls that can evolve faster with higher intelligence, that the current way under Gods ruling which is a slow, long and methodical process of evolution.

Additionally, Lucifer also proposed the concept of "karma", which is cause and effect. What you sow you reap. He sincerely believed that this will help the souls to learn and evolve faster. As talented and charming as he is, he was able to sell his concept of new creation and evolution to 1/3rd of the angels in heaven.

With 1/3rd of the angels, Lucifer waged a full-fledged war against God.

"And there was war in heaven: Michael and his angels fought against the dragon; and the dragon fought and his angels, And prevailed not; neither was their place found any more in heaven. And the great dragon was cast out, that old serpent, called the Devil, and Satan, which deceiveth the whole world: he was cast out into the earth, and his angels were cast out with him." - [Revelation 12:7-9]

God defeated Lucifer and then banished him and his followers from Heaven. And so did Lucifer Fall from grace with the utmost tragedy, horror, dismay, and terror.

He was cast to the Earth, and his angels were cast out with him. – Revelations 12:9

"And I beheld Satan fall as lightning from heaven." - Luke 10:18

The Book of Isaiah also records this event – "How you are fallen from heaven, O Lucifer, son of the morning! How you are cut down to the ground, you who weakened the nations! For you have said in your heart: 'I will ascend into heaven, I will exalt my throne above the stars of God; I will also sit on the mount of the congregation on the farthest sides of the north; I will ascend above the heights of the clouds, I will be like the Most High'" (Isaiah 14:12-14).

Devil

The devil here refers to Lucifer or Satan or both. For the purposes of this book, we will assume both Lucifer and Satan are the same beings as both have the same ideology. Both names are used interchangeably.

After the Fall

After the Fall, Lucifer and his cohorts gradually expanded their control over this section of our universe. About 200,000 years ago the rebellion entered our section of the galaxy and then Earth Many leaders of the different planets of this universe were either captured or were taken over cleverly by Lucifer. Leaders and planetary princes (a planetary prince can be likened to the president/prime minister of the planet) of more than 700 planets in our local universe bowed to Lucifer.

God and Christ saw that things were not going well for the Universe and decided to localize the

battle. This served two purposes. First to attract all darkness to the identified world(s), so the effects can be localized and the dark army's fate can be determined once and for all; secondly, the localization can prevent further dark infestation to other galaxies and universes.

Fall of Earth to Lucifer Rebellion

"Spiritual warfare is very real. There's a furious, fierce, and ferocious battle raging in the realm of the spirit between the forces of God and the forces of evil. Warfare happens every day, all the time. Whether you believe it or not, you are on a battlefield. You are in warfare." — Pedro Okoro

In the grand constellation picture, planet Earth is one of the unique shining "Pearl" created by Christ with the help of God. The illumination of the crystal blueish color is extremely eye-catching and glittering among the shining stars in the local universe. Earth attracted many space travelers to check out and set foot on the surface. Some of them were involved to set up their settlements when their "Home" planets were in "trouble". All their needs and wants were fully met and supplied without conditions. Their descendants were living without worry and with full compassion and love, walking freely with abundance while learning their lessons and experiences. All lived a high nobility life and worked toward their soul evolutionary journey.

The planetary prince of Earth at that time is Caligastia. Satan successfully swayed him to join his rebellion. They established headquarters in Mesopotamia. This is the beginning of the fall of Earth. Satan successfully breached the barrier between Hell and Earth, this signaled the beginning of the Apocalypse.

For two hundred millennia, the battle continued until it centered on our world, planet Earth.

Note: The above is a short summary of the War in Heaven, the reality of Lucifer/Satan/Devil, and how the Fall happened. If you want a thorough and detailed understanding, please check out my book "Christ vs Satan – Final Battle for Earth has Begun", which is part of "The Real Matrix Series". Will have a link at the end of this book.

Purpose of the War – For Your Soul

Now that the Earth is under the control and influence of Dark Lords, it has become a challenge for Humanity to grow spiritually and become closer to God. So God sends numerous beings over many centuries to advance the cause of Light. But what exactly do these beings of Light teach? All great teachers taught us how to grow in consciousness and become closer to God. Soul evolution. It is your soul that both Darkness and Light are after. Both Light and Dark are fighting for control of your soul, the planet, and the humans on it. This single planet can change the course of the entire war for either side.

How the War is Fought

You're surely familiar with warfare from just watching the news. Whether it's the conflict in

Ukraine as of the time of this writing, the Gulf War back in the 1990s, or the Vietnam War even earlier, you're probably familiar with the sound of gunfire, explosions, cannons, and missiles from jet planes flying overhead. But even those wars, as brutal as they were, had some rules attached to them. For instance, even though American and Soviet-backed countries fought constantly during the Cold War, neither the US nor the USSR used nuclear weapons against each other directly. The spiritual conflict between Light and Dark is a total war in the truest sense, occurring over thousands of years and on many different planes of existence. But it, too, has rules, and you must be aware of those rules to make the right choices during the conflict.

The first rule is non-interference, at least directly. Satan and his angels will not physically manifest on earth and do battle with weapons like swords and guns, and neither will the forces of Light. Combat, for now, is mostly in unseen spiritual realms, as both sides try to gain influence over particular human beings who can shape human society as a whole in ways more amenable to one side or another. However, humans can petition either side for certain types of help if they ask directly.

Humans have the freedom to contact and follow either God or Devil. Free will is the greatest gift of our creator. Some humans contact Lucifer's agents to gain knowledge of dark arts like using spells to cloud people's minds or gain social or political influence or summon demonic entities from other realms, etc. Contacting beings of Light can offer more positive effects, both personally—providing better mental health and a sense of well-being—and on a larger scale, by soothing people's minds to make them more peaceful or appealing to their better natures to give rise to positive social programs or matters like that.

The vast majority of human beings on earth are unaware of this spiritual conflict. And even those who are aware of it, like you are now, cannot see everything going on in the great Light-Dark war. While you may be able to recollect some wisdom from them under very particular circumstances, and while the virtue you display in this life has some impact, you lose virtually all of your concrete memories when you pass away. That is precisely why you should try to do the best you can in this one lifetime. You must rely on yourself to navigate the time you spend on earth that you're aware of. You can't rely on previous past glories (if you had any) to carry you. The wisdom contained in this book can help you make up for past mistakes you might have committed and set you back on the path to advancement. The Universal Father's mercy is boundless, and he wants everyone to reach him eventually, no matter how long it takes or how much difficulty they might have.

The one exception to these rules can be found in our DNA. Living in the modern world, you're probably aware of how DNA is the building block of life, the blueprints according to which our cells grow and develop, and thus the foundation of our physical bodies. However, DNA contains traces of spiritual truth as well. With special training, you can access buried memories within your DNA. It can be very hard to get full memories, so most of the time, you can only access fragments, but once you know of the existence of the spiritual matrix, and higher realms of consciousness to which you can ascend, your soul journey can be enlightening. Some of these memories in your DNA contain 'codes' for not only moral virtue and heroism in our universe, but the secrets of enlightenment and advancement towards the higher planes. This knowledge is supernatural in the truest sense— even if you had not experienced it so far, the Universal Father and his angels spread it throughout the fabric of the universe, where it became attached to certain strands of DNA. This supernatural genetic knowledge is crucial to future battles in the great war. We know there have been many battles on Earth related to suppressing the lighted DNA. The DNA wars are real. It is beyond the scope of this book to discuss these topics.

Perhaps if humanity manages to shake off the influence of the Dark entirely, the veil separating Humans and Angels can be lifted, but until then, we must wage our struggle quarantined from the rest of the universe. Yet another reason the present battle on earth is so important; either Light or Dark will win, and the prize they are after is your soul. You, as an individual, can influence how the entire universe will turn out!

The Prize: Your Soul

Lucifer does not want our bodies in and of themselves, but our minds–our souls–generate energy that his forces desperately need. The darkness feeds off negative emotional energies from humans. This makes Dark beings strong. The stronger they are, the more darkness they hold. Higher Dark entities can effortlessly subjugate a normal human being. Once you are subjugated and controlled, you become a weapon of Darkness. You are mind-controlled.

Souls are eternal and pass through time by gaining different experiences. Death of the human physical body is not the end for en-souled beings that can think. Now, the activity of the soul—that which directs us towards good, virtuous deeds (producing illuminated, holy souls) or evil ones (producing tainted, condemned souls)— creates spiritual echoes across not only this universe but all other ones, including the higher universes from which Lucifer originally came, reaching all the way to Paradise. At least, that is the case most of the time. However, the actions of souls, mediated through the physical shells they currently occupy, can be good or bad. This energy is used by either side to further the agenda.

Many creatures from all across many universes can provide spiritual energy in this way. But humans on earth, due to the intensity with which we live our lives and the strength of the beliefs we hold, consequently have strong, bright souls, which generate immense amounts of this energy. Therein lies the heart of Satan's plan. Lucifer plans to turn Earth into a gigantic prison of shadows. There, human beings will be enslaved and trapped, our souls no longer able to advance to higher universes. Our souls will be imprisoned on earth, where they will be used to fuel Lucifer and his fallen angels in their dark crusade against the Universal Father and his loyal ones. Satan needs human souls to further their agenda and cannot just annihilate us.

Light, by contrast, does not want to trap souls for selfish use—quite the opposite. The forces of Light want Earth and its human populations to evolve rather than stagnate and languish in prison. When human beings express virtue and thus ascend to higher universes or worlds on higher vibratory levels (to use technical terms), their souls emit light energy which strengthens God's forces to help free more souls and further the co-creation process. This is good for both individuals and the universe as a whole, and the souls who, have ascended to the highest vibratory level of all (Paradise) are true juggernauts in the struggle against darkness.

Thus, both sides have a very vested interest in you. Yes, you, the person reading this book right now! Your actions here and now, in this world, and the beliefs you hold, not only influence your life but the lives of others, by extension. This will ultimately influence the course of the final battle between Light and Dark–which side will your soul's energy go to? You must make the right decision.

How the Soul Evolves

To truly understand the spiritual struggle, you need to understand its relationship with the material world. To quickly review, let us go over the several parts of a full human being.

First is your physical body–This is what breathes, grows, gets healthy or sick, is made out of cells like all other creatures, and so on.

Then is the mind. This is most closely associated with the brain of the physical body, and this is what thinkers refer to when they talk about what interprets sense experience, what has emotions, what makes judgments, and so on. This is the physical aspect of what sets human beings and other sentient creatures above animals and plants.

The third is the spirit, which is partially divine. This aspect of a human being actually precedes his or her personality and becomes part of a person when they are born and start interacting with the world. It is called the "Divine Within" and helps attune human beings to the Divine Will.

Finally, we come to the soul. This is something acquired and tuned through experience. The soul is what the human spirit becomes through experience, whether choosing to conform to the Divine Will or reject it. In any case, this is the immortal part of a human being that survives his or her death.

WHY CHRIST CAME TO EARTH

In a universe as vast as ours, with all of its solar systems and galaxies, why would the Divine take such an interest in a small planet orbiting an unremarkable star at the very edge of the Milky Way?

The Order of the Universe

The Bible is certainly one of the greatest books ever written. Christians obviously find it holy, but even members of other faiths, or no faith at all, can acknowledge the power of its moral teachings and the insight it provides into transcendent reality.

As the Bible teaches, there is only one supreme God, creator of humanity, Earth itself, and the heavens above, all the stars we see in the night sky, and many more beyond. So great is God's power that he did not create a single planet, but many thousands upon thousands—so very many that human beings can scarcely conceive of such a humongous multitude. In His infinite wisdom, in order to best minister to the innumerable beings who need His guidance, God will sometimes distribute His power in the form of spiritual servants to directly oversee galaxies, then solar systems, and then individual planets with life on them.

However, while the Bible concentrates primarily on God's interactions with human beings on Earth, we are not the only ones He is concerned with. Many of the stars we see are orbited by planets, and on some of those planets, life evolved, just like it did on Earth (with Genesis being understood as an allegory for God's concern with sapient life specifically). Intelligent creatures with souls like human beings arose on an even smaller number of those planets. Though such aliens are naturally very different from us in physical shape, they are also capable of language, reasoning, and empathy for other living things, which makes them similar to us spiritually, and explains why God is concerned with them as well. In return, all the wisest and most enlightened inhabited planets of the universe also recognize and worship God, giving thanks and praise to Him in a multitude of their own ways.

By separating Himself into emissaries, and having those divine emissaries struggle through the responsibilities of overseeing galaxies, and planets, and occasionally even incarnating themselves physically to live amongst the mortals they rule, God shares the joy and pain of His creations, and thus the glory of their self-improvement as well, which does not contradict but enhances and deepens the already-existing glory of His divine nature, personality, and mode of existence.

Needless to say, it is very easy to understand how all of this would apply to Christ's appearance on Earth. God and His emissaries, being wise and caring, know they have to incarnate within a world in a material universe at precisely the right time and place, and in precisely the right social context (given the individual development of that world in terms of culture, religion and understanding of God and morality, socioeconomic factors, and so on) in order to leave the most positive impact.

For Earth, that time was 0 A.D., in the context of the Jewish people living under Roman rule in the Middle East. As the analysis of the Old Testament, we have performed earlier illustrates, the prophets and sages of Jewish history had made great strides in understanding God's will, His greatness, and the moral tenets He wanted His creations to uphold. Although cloaked in myth and allegory appropriate for a species that had not yet, at the time, created advanced science, Jewish teaching affirmed the omni-benevolence, uniqueness, and oneness of the Universal Father. The Old Testament also contained many powerful moral messages to ensure its adherents stayed on the right path: admonitions to protect orphans and widows, care for the poor, be honest and forthright in your dealings with everyone (even your enemies), and how God's mercy would always be extended to anyone who asked for it (NIV, Exodus 22:22-27).

Now, as the Bible also states, by the time Christ was born people had started to lose sight of these teachings, so to purify them and bring the people back to the most important basics (so to speak), it was just the right moment for God Himself to direct one of His emissaries to do the job personally. Also, through the strength of that emissary's preaching and teaching skills, the noble moral teachings the Jewish people had refined throughout the centuries could be spread to humanity in general through the Roman Empire, which was the largest and most far-reaching in the world at the time.

Who, exactly, was that emissary? Before He was Jesus, this individuation of the Universal Father's power was Christ (also known as Christ Michael in the higher levels of the Universe)

The Importance of Earth

You might also be wondering: Why Earth, specifically? After all, given how vast our universe is, even if its creator, there are many millions of worlds in our universe. Why did He not incarnate (or, as the technical language goes, proceed through a Bestowal) on one of those? The answer has to do with what makes human beings particularly important in the grand scheme of things.

Darkness is concentrated on Earth – What happens on Earth has ripple effects across the Universe

As we have seen before the dark forces have been quarantined to this sector of the galaxy, with Earth being the epicenter. Planer Earth is quarantined or locked-down to arrest the spread of the virus of darkness.

In higher realms, planet earth is called "The Planet of Sorrows" or "Earth Shawn". If darkness is defeated here on Earth, it is certain to be defeated and eradicated in the rest of the worlds that have been taken over by Satan.

If Christ has to save His universe, the best place to target is the epicenter of evil, planet earth.

Earth is a seed planet – A very important one

There are usually very few (probably only one or two planets in the Galaxy or the local sector of the universe) planets deemed worthy of new Soul creation. When a planet is created, all life forms are in group consciousness. In due time with training and opportunities, the life-form takes on a unique identity. When this life-form is able to make its own choices or have a "will" of its own, it then begins to form mind packets of information which evolves into what we call "Soul". Planet Earth is imbued with this unique God-given ability and so has a special place in the universe

To Free Human Souls from Prison of Darkness

Now that the Earth is under the control and influence of Dark Lords, it has become a challenge for Humanity to grow spiritually and become closer to God. So God sends numerous beings over many centuries to advance the cause of Light. But what exactly do these being of Light teach? All great teachers taught us how to grow in consciousness and become closer to God. How to evolve one's Soul to get closer to the heavenly Father.

It is your soul that both Darkness and Light are after. Both Light and Dark are fighting for control of your soul, and hence the planet. This single planet can change the course of the entire war for either side. Both God and Satan has a vested interest in your Soul.

Power of Human Emotions

Living in the modern world, everyone is familiar with power, defined in the broadest scientific sense as simply "the ability to do work." Steam power allows us to move great machines by boiling water, while nuclear power uses the energy generated by splitting atoms to do the same, or generate electricity and warmth, and so on. However, what many people are not aware of is that there is also spiritual power.

God the Father is the absolute height of spiritual power. Every sapient being in the entire universe possesses spiritual power as well. Sapience, or the ability to reason, think, and act morally, is much more than just a mundane material interaction of electrochemical stimuli. We human beings, and all the other thinking creatures on other planets, are far more than mere organic computers. Our acts of reasoning, as well as our demonstrations of benevolence, compassion, and obedience to God's laws, reflect the deeper layers of reality and thus influence those deeper layers. In other words, the experiences of thinking creatures in the material world can generate not only physical power but spiritual power as well.

Now, everyone knows that there are very many differentiations in the amount of physical power various systems generate. A steam engine, despite being very powerful and top of the line in the eighteenth century, does not generate as much power as a coal plant, and even those are less efficient and powerful (and worse for the environment barring catastrophes, to boot) than the most modern nuclear power plants, with fusion technology promising to generate even more. The same applies to spiritual power. For a variety of reasons too complex to describe in depth, human beings, out of all the beings in the universe, produce the highest amount of spiritual power per capita over the course of our lifetimes. Our emotions are so strong, the struggles we endure (and overcome) so grave, that our souls (those spiritual and mental parts that distinguish sapient material beings from mere animals) leave larger ripples in the etheric and astral levels of this universe than those of worlds elsewhere in the universe.

This spiritual power can be harnessed toward a multitude of different ends. The forces of Light, following the will of the Universal Father, would use it for good. God's desire for humans, as well as all mortal beings, is that they do good work over the course of their mortal lifespans, enhancing the positivity and purging the negativity in their souls. Death is not the end for sapient, soulful beings. In the ordinary course of things, if we have lived good lives and pursued wisdom and Godliness after we die, our mortal bodies may be gone but our souls remain, ascending towards higher spiritual levels, drawing closer to the Universal Father. As long as we uphold virtue and obey God's teaching, every life we pass brings us closer and closer to our ultimate goal of full communion with God. And this process, the ascendance of souls, produces a huge amount of spiritual power, with the ascendance of human souls producing the very highest amount possible in this universe.

Such positive "light" energy, in spiritual terms, allows higher spiritual beings to carry out their will—to perform more actions across a further span of time and space and within a shorter period of time. Thus can they generate more worlds, spend more time guiding and uplifting the residents of already existing worlds, refine the evolutionary processes of the worlds under their oversight, and so on.

Obviously, this process requires us to have a good grasp of morality and spiritual issues. And who better to teach us about them than a divine being

Himself? Thus, Christ chose exactly the right time and place to restore the truths ancient Jews had previously discovered, incorporate them into even higher teachings, and spread them throughout the Roman empire, where they would remain established across the world. For the peoples of Earth, this would help them live better lives and ascend more easily to higher levels, and for the rest of the universe, would thus provide more spiritual energy for higher beings to perform good works. A win-win situation indeed!

Christ Bestowal on Planet Earth

Planet Earth is absolutely central to the battle between Light and Dark due to the comparatively massive amount of spiritual energy human beings produce. And while the struggle was slow, Lucifer was slowly but surely gaining the upper hand through a variety of means. His agents surreptitiously eliminated Light bloodlines on Earth, subverted the noble teachings of many great philosophers like Aristotle or Zoroaster, and placed merciless conquerors in positions of power (across the Roman empire, for instance) to keep humanity mired in war and oppression, preventing many of us from ascending and growing closer to the Light. It was getting harder and harder for agents of Light to access the planet, very few people could commune with the Universal Father at all, and the Dark had succeeded in turning many unfortunate human souls into perpetual energy batteries, fueling the campaign against God. These troubling developments drew the attention of not just God but the highest of His angels who had been charged with overseeing our universe.

This process became harder on Earth due to the spiritual isolation or quarantine Earth is subjected to. On the other hand, the forces of Light absolutely could not allow Earth to fall into the Dark, or else everything would be lost. Thus, Christ embarked upon the riskiest and most dangerous plan imaginable for an angel of his stature. He would undergo Bestowal and use all of his energies to penetrate the Matrix. However, due to the extreme cost of that procedure, Christ would appear on Earth not as a full-grown adult, but as a humble child, profoundly vulnerable to the many Dark forces seeking his destruction!

This was essentially Christ first coming. This was a complete secret mission between God and Christ, and not even the angles and arch angels in Paradise were aware. Only after His birth as a helpless small baby, the announcement went out to the entire headquarters of the universe in heavenly realms. Many were surprised as He did not bestow with powers intact but as a helpless babe. And yes, the baby is subjected to all rules of limited consciousness of the war-torn planet.

While there are many ways the first-coming mission can be interpreted, the primary purpose is to help light win the war and pave the way for Human salvation.

For Christ, the rewards were worth the risks. If he managed to grow to adulthood on Earth, this Bestowal would prove for all time that he was truly a gifted creator and administrator and that he deserved to be sovereign over his universe for all eternity. And not only that, but success in this mission would pave the way for Light's victory, as it would undo much of the progress Dark had made in subverting human society and turning people into Dark batteries. Indeed, such a triumph would liberate not only Earth, but also several nearby star systems whose inhabitants were not as important–in terms of energy generated–as humans, but who had nevertheless been conquered by Darkness. This would lead to a cascade effect, where the Devil's forces would subsequently grow weaker day after day, and the forces of Light grow stronger at the same rate, allowing a swift end to the entire Rebellion after the final battle on Earth. So incredibly important was this operation that it was kept secret from even the other angels. No one knew what God and Christ were planning until he had arrived— or more accurately, been born—on Earth!

WHY DOES SATAN WANT CHRIST ON HIS SIDE

S atan is aware of Jesus' Divine status and wants to get to him before Jesus becomes fully conscious and enlightened. By getting Christ on their side, Satan thought they would have won a big, arguably crucial battle that could turn the tide of the entire war against the Light and in favor of the Dark. With Christ's incredible power, intelligence, and speaking abilities, He would have gained millions upon millions of followers and turned them towards evil ends rather than the will of the Universal Father. Rather than bringing peace and virtue into the world, the followers of a corrupted Christ would have turned it entirely over to the Dark. They would have captured governments and spread their dominion over all of Earth, making humans the latest conquered slave species to labor for Satan's evil plans. This would have provided the forces of Darkness with more spiritual energy than they ever had before (to be discussed in a later Chapter), allowing them to spread beyond Earth, perhaps through the entire universe. The Dark could then challenge God and undo their initial defeat during the Fall.

The darkness as cunning as they were, thought they had chosen the perfect moment to win another convert to their dark cause on that fateful day nearly two thousand years ago. They were not entirely wrong to think so. It is a testament to both Christ's strength and the foresight of the Universal Father that their plans were foiled. Once again, it is difficult to directly analyze the plots of Darkness, but these are some hypotheses our most advanced scholars have put forward to explain the behavior of these Dark leaders.

First, Jesus had not performed any miracles yet. As discussed in the sections on His life above, Jesus was a very precocious, insightful, and wise child, with a very close and special relationship with the Universal Father. As an adolescent and young adult, He continued to 'wow' everyone around Him with His maturity, good judgment, work ethic, and so on, as well as His piety and knowledge of religious matters. However, aside from His family—who knew of His supernatural destiny thanks to messages from angels—the world, in general, had not yet caught on to the fact that Christ was explicitly divine, not just an excellent teacher.

Now, if Christ had started performing miracles already, it would have been too late to turn Him over to the dark side. His status as an emissary, servant, and representative of the Light would have already been solidified and it would have been nearly impossible to subvert such a well-established personality. By getting to Him before He had a chance to really get steady on His feet, so to speak, the Dark leaders hoped that His entire ministry would begin dedicated to the Dark rather than the Light, thus bringing all of his future accomplishments into the fold of the former.

Second, Jesus had not yet become very popular, nor had His public ministry really taken off. As mentioned above, He had many friends, and His customers very much appreciated His skilled carpentry and management. But He was not a famous celebrity, much less the world-famous figure He would end up as. At the time of His sojourn to Mount Hermon, He was still a fairly obscure Jewish citizen, not so different from millions of others at the time. By getting to Him before he grew famous, Satan wagered He would be able to bring millions of new servants of the Dark into the fold. On the other hand, if they had waited until after He became well known, the audience He cultivated would necessarily have been much less receptive to the lies of the Dark, since if Christ had taught them Light precepts but suddenly changed after being caught by evil, they would realize something was wrong. Thus, the only way for Christ to really fulfill the plots of Darkness would be if He were already one of them before His ministry began.

Spiritual beings of both the Light and Dark can recognize beings of a higher order through their spiritual signatures, not just by their mundane physical appearances. Thus, the forces of Dark knew that the man at Mount Hermon was more than just a simple hermit. Christ probably had a glow around Him, perhaps imperceptible to normal human eyes but very evident to Satan. There is also evidence to indicate that Jesus had heavenly visitors who manifested and un-manifested at certain points during his solitude. Satan would have been aware of this.

Satan's Perceived Advantages, Christ's True Strengths

Satan almost certainly thought he had overwhelming advantages when they tried to tempt Christ. When he spied on Mount Hermon, it would have seemed to him that Jesus was struggling both physically and emotionally. Physically, because He had not had much to eat. It would have been harsh for Christ to have endured sleeping out in the wilderness. Emotionally, Christ would have seemed troubled due to the privations of solitude. Even though, as described above, loneliness can strengthen one's soul, it's still a very difficult thing to be separated from your friends and family for so long, especially for 40 days. Thus, Satan likely wagered that Christ would be weak and desperate, and thus open to honeyed lies from the Darkness.

In such a state, Satan figured that Christ would be very confused. One's physical state affects one's mental state, after all. If Christ was very hungry and physically deprived, especially if He had been hurt by the elements on Mount Hermon, He would have been less focused, His grasp on virtue and God's moral principles less firm, and less able to distinguish between virtuous spirits who wanted to help Him and evil ones from Satan sent to deceive Him. In other words, Christ would have seemed like perfect prey for a subtle spiritual attack, not just a physical one.

The devil could have compared Christ to one of the many prophets. Keep in mind that every prophet born before Jesus came with a message that almost always fell on the deaf ears of the Israelites. He had sized Jesus up so that, just like the former ones, he would go about with God's plans while arranging his death. Just like the prophets came, and the old testament of the Bible has it on record that the Jews were already renowned for killing their prophets because of the kind of heart they possessed, he had rounded off Jesus. He had felt it would not be different from the other prophets who had come before him.

Finally, Satan believed that Christ would have been operating with just His human ego alone. Human minds are more advanced than those of any other creature on Earth, but we are still very primitive on spiritual levels. Even for the wisest and most learned among us, it is difficult to really grasp and hold to the tenets of the Universal Father's law, to acknowledge our own limitations and humbly learn from higher agents, and indeed to even acknowledge higher spiritual realities in the first place. If Christ had been limited in such ways, He would have been easily misled by spiritual attacks. This was just what Satan was counting on.

- **Christ's inner world is completely different from His external appearance:** Yes, He was a handsome and healthy youth, and outwardly, He didn't look very different from other Jews of the time. But as true scholars know, outward physical appearance counts for very little. Christ's inner self, His spiritual and mental levels, were far, far beyond what even the most beautiful or handsome physical form would indicate.

- **Christ had direct inner communion with the Universal Father:** Satan might have seen Him praying, but they weren't aware of how Christ connected to God on an even deeper level, far more than ordinary people could even dream of doing. Thus, Christ's connection to God was much, much stronger than Satan could have ever anticipated, and his attempts to tempt him were thus nowhere near sufficient to break such a powerful bond.

- **Christ derived strength from within:** There is no strength that is like the one we draw from within us. There is always a knowing from within that asserts our essence as we go through life. The strength that never fails comes from our Spirit; it gives us directions from time to time on whether to do one thing or the other. Satan could scarcely comprehend the thinking and attitudes of one as attuned to virtue and righteousness as Christ was. They thought mortals and spiritual beings alike only grew strong from external factors, either wealth and power or dominating or enslaving others. They never considered that Christ had a limitless source of strength and resilience in His inner self, which He had assiduously cultivated over the course of His life and most notably during His period of solitude on Mount Hermon.

On that note, Satan thought Christ could only have been weakened physically and emotionally through solitude. He did not consider the advantages of loneliness we discussed above, how Christ gained greater perspective, self-knowledge, self-reliance, and so on. It is easy to understand by thinking of popular stories today. Just about every superhero has to spend time by themselves, such as Bruce Wayne, as Batman, fighting crime without any help before Alfred and Robin came into his life, or Superman retreating to his Fortress of Solitude deep in the Arctic. The darkness never realized that Christ was strengthened in important ways by His sojourn even as He had to deal with its difficulties.

WHAT HAPPENED IN THE WILDERNESS?

I t was one of the greatest battles in the history of humanity and the planet Earth itself. The fate of Earth, and many worlds beyond it, hinged upon its outcome. Yet it was not fought with swords and shields, nor bullets and tanks. One side did not even take up arms. It was not a physical struggle. And most of all, absolutely no one except its participants witnessed its progress and ultimate outcome, even though all of history would have been radically different if the other side had won.

It was rather a struggle purely on the moral plane—the temptation of Christ, where the forces of Darkness tried and failed to turn our Savior over to them and convince Him to reject the Universal Father. It is certainly good they failed or else we likely wouldn't be here—or we would perhaps be suffering fates worse than death! But how did this moral struggle play out? It is easy to visualize great battles with weapons and soldiers, but a purely spiritual conflict seems a great deal harder to wrap one's head around. This chapter will tell you everything you need to know about the temptation of Christ.

Testing is part of the process of the Spiritual Journey

Every human being, young and old, male or female, from any part of the world, has to deal with challenges in their life. We all also have to make choices and, in many cases, resist temptation. Sometimes we have to choose between an action pleasurable in the short-term and another more profitable in the long-term, or between actions that could hurt others but benefit us personally, or those which require sacrifice on our part but benefit society as a whole. The most significant and best-remembered stories often involve choices like these, and these themes also show up in the great religions of the world, capturing universal truths as they do.

Testing is important for one's soul because it proves you have truly learned all you can on the lower levels, thus allowing you to move on to higher consciousness levels safely. Again, take the analogy of a high school or college course. You certainly wouldn't take the final exam on the very first day of class, but you wouldn't take it even in the first week or month either. Instead, you'd first take smaller quizzes, and then a midterm, only building up to the final exams gradually. The same applies to spiritual matters. First, your soul undergoes minor trials, with the hope that you will learn and grow from them. Finally, at the very end, you will have to endure a "Dark Night of the Soul", all by yourself, with no aid or assistance this time, in order to demonstrate you've truly internalized all the lessons of your previous struggles and can apply those lessons in a coherent and cumulative way. Christ's spiritual test on Hermon was the greatest of this kind imaginable. Instead of just struggling with internal vices like most humans do in their soul journeys, He faced down the leaders of darkness themselves, drawing upon the lessons He had gained from childhood and young manhood—the love of His parents and friends, His struggles with smaller physical inconveniences like stomach ailments or falling down, and so on—and proved he could utilize all those lessons in an arena where God was on the sidelines

All in all, this was Christ's personal test to prove Him to be a worthy Creator Son and ruler over the entire universe. This sort of thing is analogous to the smaller tests all human beings go through, both in mundane terms and higher spiritual ones. When you're in school, you're expected to pass your math, history, and other courses with tests and exams, which you have to take all by yourself with no external aid. Someone helping you during the test itself, or you looking at someone else's answers, would be cheating! The same applies to a spiritual journey. When you want to demonstrate the advancement of your intellectual and moral abilities, you have to do so entirely on your own, without any direct aid from God or higher spiritual entities, to prove that you are the one who has advanced and that you, on your own, are capable of advanced spiritual work, rather than needing to rely on others all the time. Only then will you be permitted to grow to higher planes of consciousness.

Soul progression happens only with testing

Just as students go from one class to the other through passing examinations, life will always bring tests to us when it is time for us to move forward. Tests are not something that our fleshly nature wants, there is always a conflict between our body and the structures that God had prepared for our progressions and achievements in life. It is another way of building and strengthening us from within. The universe is always in a conspiracy for our growth.

Passing spiritual tests with little or no support

There are times when loyalty to God will be driven out from within us. Even for Jesus Christ, there needed to be pressure upon the flesh to drive out the possibilities of the Spirit. It might not be suitable to go through trials and difficulties in life, but it is a sure way to help us realize the possibilities that are secretly embedded in us. The same applied to Christ, though it was much more significant for Him than it would be for an ordinary person taking the SATs or something, of course.

For Christ's test on Mount Hermon, at the moment of Satan's temptation, the Universal

Father temporarily left Him, as did all the guardian angels who were protecting Him previously. In that sense, Christ was totally alone, as one might have to take the SATs alone. However, Christ was not left entirely powerless. His spirit had certain kinds of astral and etheric protection in place that the guardian angels had left behind so that the forces of Darkness could not use any unfair methods to simply mind-control Him or bend Him to their will. But aside from that, He had nothing except His own wisdom and knowledge of God to refute the lies of the darkness.

Evolved beings usually have suffered more

Some people love to put it as suffering while others love to put it as challenges; whichever way you put it, they are like the grease that makes our movement easy from one stage of purpose fulfillment to the other. This is proof that the wisdom of God is foolishness to man, we don't want to suffer, and we don't like having challenges. We are not happy when we are being tried, we respond by crying, and some of us even tend to blame God for our ordeals. Leaving God to seek help from other means is the worst-case scenario. Challenges are promotions in disguise; only those who have been through one can understand. Even nature explains to us how important it is to suffer before we eventually begin to bear fruits. It has been proven by many lives also that the deeper the suffering is, the greater the glory to come. This is why we must not compare ourselves with anyone irrespective of how close we are to them.

A superhero journey

Can you imagine any real superhero who did not go through their Dark Night of the Soul? I do not think there is any.

What qualifies a superhero? When you hear the word superhero, you might look at some who have all the material, but superheroes are those who have been tested and proven. A superhero is known for how many inner battles he has conquered and how he has been able to find strength from within to stand for the truth even if there are a lot of pressures around. Superheros are known for their maturity, resilience, strength, and many other virtues that have been gained during tests. Everyone goes through dark nights, but how we deal with them or our actions makes our character and hence shapes our destiny.

Universe Trial

Christ closed Himself off spiritually to all other distractions, but for only communion with The Father. He went through five weeks of intense training. This was His "Dark Night of the Soul". What exactly the training entails in this five weeks is not generally public knowledge at this time and is beyond the scope of discussion for this short book.

After five weeks of this training, despite the hunger His human body endured, Jesus was more assured and self-confident than ever before. He knew He had gained as much wisdom and understanding as it was possible to acquire on the mortal plane of this universe, and was certain he had triumphed over the most basic material levels of this particular personality manifestation in this specific region of space-time.

In the sixth week of the journey, the very last, Jesus knew it was time for his greatest trial. This event in the universal records came to be known as the "Universe Trail". This was the very reason He has chosen to come to this planet.

At the end of his self-imposed exile, he opened Himself spiritually to worldly distractions. The leaders of the Darkness, Satan, and his allies descended physically to Mount Hermon and could be seen with the naked eye by Jesus. They also sent many of their demonic servants physically to attack and harass Him.

Satan and his allies were able to manifest and un-manifest their body in physical form, meaning they had a body form and the knowledge to use this body form. However, Jesus' body form is limited to physical form and does not have the ability to manifest and un-manifest at will in the physical realm. This is important to know because Dark forces had greater power to affect material beings. However, they were not able to cause harm to Jesus, as he is protected and also has the 'awareness' and abilities to protect himself.

After the demons could not even come close to breaking Christ physically or mentally, Satan tried to subvert Christ spiritually, through the temptations described in the Bible.

Indeed, the temptation itself recapitulated the slow increase of difficulty one might experience in the aforementioned examples, but this time pertaining to levels of spirit and mind in addition to the complexity of the subject matter. It is not an accident that Satan posed precisely three questions to Christ. These questions were designed to test the multiple components of the soul, starting with the lowest human ego first, and then going from that to the higher self. The devil knew what he wanted to achieve, but had to be cunning because that is his nature. The test he put Christ through was to prove that no man was above mistakes and that Jesus Christ was also subject to the flesh.

Satan is aware of Christ's divine status. However, Satan thinks that Christ does not know Himself. So he prefixed the questions with "If you are the Son of God" for the first two questions. Also, Satan thought that the person on the mountain does not know him, so in the last question when Christ answered by calling Satan by name, Satan's cover is blown off.

Test-1: Testing physical body weakness, immediate human gratification with physical food.

And the tempter came and said to him, "If you are the Son of God, command these stones to become loaves of bread." – Mathew 4:3

Tempting Christ with bread—was purely physical, and measured His resistance to immediate gratification. This is the lowest, most animalistic part of the human psyche. After all, even the most basic animals incapable of any sort of higher thought, like slugs or sessile creatures like coral, still need food in the form of nutrition. This was accordingly the easiest test to pass for any enlightened creature, since control over one's bodily functions and urges is one of the first things required to pass from infancy to childhood to adulthood, and thus one of the first marks of true sapience. Jesus was too savvy for this ploy.

He replied, "It is written: 'Man shall not live on bread alone, but on every word that comes from the mouth of God.'" – Mathew 4:4

Test-2: Testing of divine nature - If he jumped from a cliff, will angels catch him?

"If you are the Son of God, throw yourself down, for it is written, "'He will command his angels concerning you,' and "'On their hands they will bear you up, lest you strike your foot against a stone.'" - Mathew 4:6

The test is challenging Christ to attempt suicide so that angels would assumedly rescue Him, reflecting a high level of human consciousness: our ability to trust in God. Lower animals do not truly understand the existence of higher spiritual realities, though they do have a vague awareness of them (see, for instance, how dogs often seem sensitive to ghosts and demons). Only rational creatures, most notable humans on Earth, are capable of consciously acknowledging God's existence and carrying out His will. In Christ's case, His divine nature would have also reflected His knowledge of divine commands, so this was a test for that supernaturally high level of Christ's spirit, which most human beings in ordinary life lack. The fact that Christ did not feel the need to jump from the top of the temple proved He had total trust and faith in God, and thus proved He was entirely aware of His true nature, His mission, and the ultimate good that would come of God's plans.

Jesus maintained his integrity and responded by quoting scripture, saying, "It is said, Thou shalt not tempt the Lord thy God.'" - Matthew 4:7

Test-3: Testing of Human Ego, Power - Satan offers Christ to become the prince of the planet if he bows

Satan has the power to manifest and unmanifest at will. Satan led Jesus to the highest point in the land, Mount Hermon, and with his supernatural powers, showed Him in a single instant every kingdom on Earth that existed at the moment and would exist in the future.

Satan told Jesus, "I will give you all their authority and splendor; it has been given to me, and I can give it to anyone I want to. If you worship me, it will be all yours."

The test involved a higher level of human consciousness as well: Our desire for power, influence, and fame, which is an outgrowth of our nature as social creatures, or our human ego. The natural man is prone to pride and creates in all of us a desire for recognition, power, and riches. Not only do these seem to provide easy solutions to life's many problems, but they also seem to fill our need to feel important and loved. Individuals, families, and nations have gone to the ends of the earth and their beliefs to earn more money and gain more glory. The test for power comes to every man in life. It does not matter who that man is; as long as one is human, there will always be a need to acquire or fight for power. Power is in different phases and various parts of life. There is the power to rule; there is power brought about by monetary possessions, there is power brought about by intellectualism, and all forms of power are worth fighting for. Power makes everyone around us see us as important, and after acquiring everything we need, the quest for power is a natural feeling that comes to us; the ability to make sure that we do not become too obsessive about it is what we all need as humans. It is a natural thing to desire power, but time and conditions are what help us to decipher whether it is right for us or not.

The very lowest creatures do not possess egos because they have no social relations at all. Slugs live more and less by themselves, except for mating, and they do not form parental bonds, they just leave their eggs where they lay them. Coral and other sessile creatures can't move or experience things at all, so naturally, they do not possess anything even close to an ego. Animals that live in herds and flocks, where they have to help each other survive, are more complex and thus have primitive egos, but the ego is most thoroughly developed in humankind, where we must always navigate the complexities of human society: worrying about how various groups perceive us, our material standing in relation to those groups, what courtesy requires towards all of them, and so on. Because of these social relations, we are always thinking about fame and power, and that is the biggest challenge for our ego; we must learn to subsume such 'egoistic' desire to our faith in God.

Christ succeeded perfectly in this. Becoming prince of Earth, as Satan offered, would be nearly irresistible to the social ego on its own, but Christ knew better and promptly refused Satan's offer with His apt and witty response

"Away from me, Satan! For it is written: 'Worship the Lord your God, and serve him only.' – Mathew 4:10

The Aftermath of Satan's Tests

Some of us might wonder why Satan stopped after just three questions. He is certainly a persistent and devious Lord of Darkness, after all. Would he really have given up so easily? And were there really only three temptations that could have possibly worked against Christ?

Perhaps Christ put a stop to all of Satan's schemes (at that moment) with His answer to the third question. Christ ended the whole conversation with "Away from me, Satan!" implying that Christ recognized Satan and commanded authoritatively. This must have been a shock to Satan as he did not expect it."

If the only thing Christ said was 'no' that probably would have encouraged Satan to keep going, dragging out the test longer than it needed to be. But with an authoritative statement of God's ultimate lordship, Christ proved there was nothing those two could possibly say to convince Him. That would have been enough to get Satan to shut up and realize that the Dark had thoroughly lost that battle.

Now, the Bible does not record what Satan said in response to that. Luke only states that the devil "left him until an opportune time" (NIV Luke 4:13). Perhaps Satan simply fled, struck speechless and in utter fear by the glory of the Lord. However, it is more likely that Satan left Christ with an "open invitation," given that he was said to have been waiting for an opportune time in the future. In other words, Satan might have said something like, "We will always be ready for you if you choose to join us in the future." Even if he failed at the moment, Satan probably hoped that the subversion would succeed at a later date, if he managed to sow doubt into Christ's heart. That obviously did not happen, and again, this is complete speculation due to the dangers of research into Dark plans and motives.

There may well be many other possibilities, but these hypotheses are intended simply to expand the reader's horizons and make him or her think, not proclaim unshakeable religious truth.

Overall, this was a massive blow to Darkness' plans and a strong repudiation of the dark manifesto. Without Christ on their side, Satan and his dark minions no longer had any hope of drawing Earth into their orbit entirely unopposed, though they would of course continue to subvert it over the millennia. However, with Christ spreading His moral teachings far and wide, their attempts would be greatly stymied. By the same token, Christ's loyalty to God disproved many elements of Satan's manifesto, such as his claims that the Universal Father was not fit to rule, that the residents of the universe should not follow Him and should instead focus on service to self rather than others—though of course under Satan's dominion anyways.

By rejecting Satan's temptations without any help or external influences, Jesus proved that the path of righteousness, narrow though it may be, could still triumph and, thus, that Satan's promises of freedom and 'self-determination' from God's rule were empty and false.

Return from the Wilderness

And as we have seen, Christ rejected every one of the temptations the evil forces threw at Him. Thanks to that, when the evil ones were finally forced to flee at the end of the sixth week, the entire universe recognized that Christ and only Christ were worthy to lead it.

Satan's great, sneaky plan had failed utterly, and he had to retreat from Earth in rage and shame. He certainly did not give up: Luke notes he left Jesus "until an opportune time," and indeed we know now that he is still carrying out spiritual warfare and all sorts of sly machinations to undermine Christ and the Father's will, and to also lead humanity into darkness, to this very day. Nevertheless, in that particular moment in time over two thousand years ago, Satan found he had nothing more in his bag of tricks that could possibly separate Christ and the Father, thus allowing the forces of Light to enjoy a well-earned victory. Indeed, even though he had been starving for forty days, Christ returned from Mount Hermon rejuvenated and even more powerful than before; Luke describes Him returning to Galilee "in the power of the Spirit," where the entire region started talking about Him and praising His wisdom and power (NIV, Luke 4:14 – 30).

By staying loyal to the will of His Father, Christ showed that it was possible for individuals of goodwill to stand up for what is right and spurn the false and selfish promises Dark tricksters offer. He proved He was capable of administering the universe justly and kindly, without concern for His own self-interest, and thus protecting all

of its residents from Lucifer/Satan's rebellion—
and any future rebellions that may occur.

Basking in the glow of victory, Christ went down from Mount Hermon. He met the boy who helped Jesus prior to his journey up the mountain. He told him only one important sentence:

"The period of rest is over, I must return to my Father's business!"

The boy understood that Christ's mission now took Him far beyond what a normal human being could endure.

Jesus Himself had definitely changed: In addition to His newfound confidence, He was much quieter, almost silent when He was not preaching because the duties as a protector of the entire universe weighed so heavily on Him. He began the next phase of the Father's plan for the salvation of Earth—and by extension all of the Universe.

SON OF MAN BECOMES SON OF GOD

The testing marked the end of His purely human career and the beginning of the more divine phase of His Bestowal.

Ending and New Beginning

Previously, as mentioned, Christ had not performed any miracles or demonstrated any spiritual powers, even though He could have if He wanted to. Only after proving Himself to be a worthy universal ruler, by His lonely resistance against Darkness, did He also prove worthy to demonstrate supernatural power (granted by

God) to the rest of humanity, because at that point He had shown He would only lead humans on the right path.

Thus was it necessary for Christ to make His conscious decision to reject Satan and obey God entirely of His own volition; it would have been meaningless if God or guardian angels had remained with Him during the temptation, because of their presence, even if they didn't say anything, would have subtly tipped the scales, and Christ wouldn't have been able to say that He achieved victory all by Himself. No one is an exception to that process, not even a Creator Son of the universe. It is absolutely necessary to learn and progress by yourself. As the old saying goes, there are no shortcuts, and for the same reason, there are no magic wands for soul evolution. You simply have to do the work and endure great hardships, but just as it was worth it for Christ in the end, it can be worth it for you as well.

Think about popular culture. Most of the time, the strongest and most evolved beings we see in our stories and TV shows are those who have suffered the most. Think about Batman, who lost his parents, or Superman, who lost his entire home world. Similarly, these heroes had to undergo a period of solitary—and often draining, soul-searching before finally reaching the level of certitude, focus, and self-confidence they needed to reach their potential. Superman had to undergo trials and spend time alone, grappling with himself, before talking to his adoptive parents and choosing to fight for Earth. Batman had to spend a long while in his mansion by himself pondering questions of law and justice before finally having the inspiration to become a masked vigilante. Christ had to go through a similar process on Mount Hermon.

Son of Man becomes Son of God

When Christ went up the mountain:

- He was a Son of Man when he walked up the mountain with all limitations and fragileness of human
- He was confused and not sure what God wanted of Him
- He was in deep introspection
- He did not know how and when to start his public mission
- He was introverted and not able to share His Father, the divine with-in message, and good news with others
- He had a lot of questions about his divine nature and the purpose of his bestowal

- He knew He had to face the dark lord head-on that ravaged His creation. He was fragile and unsure of how things would unfold

When Christ came down the mountain:

- He is completely sure of Himself and of what God wanted from Him
- He is no longer in deep introspection
- He knew that it is time for Him to start his mission in the public
- He got all answers to all his questions about his divine nature and the purpose of his bestowal
- He came back fully confident, basking in the glory of God and with great power and authority over the entire planet and the entire universe
- He is now ready to share His Father, the divine with-in message, and good news to all who have ears to hear
- He successfully defeated the dark Lord and displaced the dark planetary prince.

Spreading of Gospel

The Gospels of the Bible give us a good idea of what happened following the temptation. Filled with "the power of the Spirit"—meaning full confidence in His mission, full knowledge of God's plans, and full permission to begin preaching to the masses and displaying His awesome supernatural power—Christ left Mount Hermon and went back into the world. People all over the region of Galilee heard the news of a powerful, virtuous young preacher, and flocked to the various synagogues and public squares where He ministered.

He astonished the crowds with His expert knowledge of ancient Hebrew scripture and practice, and bested many skeptics in debate, winning further converts. He brought the war directly to the forces of the Dark, displaying His divine power by casting out demons, purifying many souls and easing their way to ascension, and destroying several hotspots of Dark spiritual activity. He cured the sick, materialized food out of thin air to feed the needy (His famous miracle of the fish and the loaves of bread), restored sight to the blind, and walked on water. This was truly when the Son of Man became the Son of God— that is to say when Christ moved beyond things humans could do (even though He was already more virtuous and wiser than most humans) to supernatural feats that were only possible by one who had transcended material limitations and received full access to the higher realities of the Universal Father.

He experienced some opposition due to the pure goodness of His preaching. At that time, many Jews and Gentiles in the area, particularly the Pharisees, had lost sight of the ancient wisdom of their ancestors. They had forgotten the commandments of Abraham and Moses and lost sight of serving the Universal Father above all. They were more concerned with their own fame and prestige among men, and often with money and power, which were precisely the temptations Jesus had risen above during His test on Hermon. Thus, Jesus went around correcting these people, sometimes harshly, as was the case when He drove the money changers out of a temple, and when he showed that some interpretations of Mosaic law were too harsh, as when He told an adulterous woman not to be stoned to death by other sinners, but also that she should "go and sin no more."

The moral teachings He espoused ensured the cause of Light would survive on Earth for generations, no matter how much effort Satan and other Dark generals put into corrupting the planet. They were absolutely furious! By preaching love and forgiveness, as He did in the Sermon on the Mount, Jesus offered humanity a degree of resistance to greed and spite, which Darkness relied upon to win converts.

Christ becomes Planetary Prince

Following Christ's victory, there were also a variety of changes made to the structure and organization of this universe itself. First, the aforementioned Caligastia (Satan's accomplice) was formally removed as the Planetary Prince of Earth. Even though he had long been subverted by Satan, the Universal Father and the other governors of the Universe had not explicitly moved against this dark lord. They knew of his plans and his betrayal of the Light, of course, but they allowed him to rule over Earth's spiritual affairs and took no action even as he spread darkness over the world, albeit gradually, since he did not have support from other loyal residents of the universe who had not been subverted. It seems strange, but this was likely in keeping with the plans of Light in the long term. Their reasoning was that if Darkness invested more in Earth for a time under Satan, they would end up losing even more if the existing rule was disrupted.

This was a defining moment as this incident gave temporary victory to light over the dark. The reigning planetary prince of Earth was cast out of his throne. Satan's accomplice Caligastia is no longer the planetary prince. Christ additionally took over the role of the planetary prince. The Bible verse states this:

"Now is the judgment of this world; now shall the prince of this world be cast down." – John 12:31
And then still nearer the completion of His lifework, He announced,

"The prince of this world is judged." - John 16:11
Christ became the planetary prince and sole commander of Earth as well as all universe. Earth would become a throne world of Light, once final victory is achieved. By dethroning the prince of darkness, Christ took Earth out of the hands of darkness; even though they still controlled much of it, it was now contested and they had to spend a great deal of time and resources trying to regain the domination they once had, which vastly delayed their plans for expansion. This was a setback for darkness. But it gave the forces of Light just enough time to hold on until they could build up their power and take the fight directly to the Dark Lord.

Now, even though the Dark had got its tendrils sunk deeply into Earth's evolution, they were cut off from their primary leader and organizer, and thus many Dark plots fell into chaos (and some were out-rightly destroyed) when Christ ascended to the position of Planetary Prince. Satan and his dark armies had to spend a great deal of time rebuilding the networks of Darkness they had previously constructed. This meant they could store up fewer resources for the final battle that would be fought millennia later, during Christ's second coming.

The last thing you need to know is that Christ did not remain a Planetary Prince forever. After Christ's ascension, he made way for Melchizedek to assume the role of Planetary Prince, while Christ reclaimed his sovereign authority over the entire universe. From that point up to today, Christ is the absolute ruler of the whole universe, organizing this plane of reality with skill and justice, while the loyal Melchizedek would handle affairs on Earth, doing his best to keep Satan and darkness from making too much progress on this world again. While Melchizedek alone would not be able to completely halt Satan's counterattacks and further attempts here on Earth, he can at least buy our world enough time to avoid complete defeat until Christ returns again for the final battle.

All power over the universe is given to Christ

After ascension from planet Earth, Christ sat on the right hand of GOD the Father. Christ had become the absolute sovereign and ruler of the universe all of the heavens and earth. However, this would not have been possible if Christ turned over to Darkness.

Temporarily arrest the spreading of darkness

Additionally, and perhaps more importantly, this threw a huge wrench in the dark lord's plans to spread Darkness in other parts of the universe. He had initially been planning to use Earth as a staging point: By subverting Christ and then spreading the tenets of Darkness and the Lucifer Manifesto across the planet, all of the souls of humanity could soon be harnessed to provide spiritual energy for Lucifer, allowing him to spread more propaganda to corrupt other worlds as well as other spiritual beings, as well as generate more evil soldiers for use in the spiritual war across the universe.

Karma - Effects lessened

This is a very complex topic and sticky to most people. I have discussed this a bit more in other books. Briefly stated here. Lucifer/Satan created the concept of Karma as implemented on planet Earth after the fall and takeover of planet Earth. According to the Dark Manifesto, everyone should ascend together or no one ascends to higher consciousness which is opposite to the light manifesto which says any person who is ready can ascend to a higher level of consciousness. Since darkness had complete control of the earth, they implemented their manifesto by creating a process by which a soul re-incarnates over and over again learning from its mistakes. This implementation has become a prison for the souls who are trapped.

The victory of Christ over Satan essentially dismantled the "prison" for souls. However, we are not totally out of the woods yet. There is some more work that needs to be accomplished that will truly make our planet a "freedom" planet. What exactly is needed to be done? Again this is beyond the scope of this book. I have discussed these aspects in book-2 of "The Real Matrix", Christ vs Satan – The Second Coming of Christ. Please check it out if interested to learn more about the real reasons and agenda of Christ's second coming.

Way of Salvation Established

Indeed, in general Christ's triumph paved the way for the faster ascension of human souls in general, even aside from the advantage gained by destroying or at least loosening the hold of Darkness on Earth. On a purely mundane level, the example of Christ himself gave people an exemplar they could point to for moral behavior. It's one thing to hear the stories and moral teachings of the Old Testament, but it's another thing to see them actually lived. This first-hand experience with virtue made it much more accessible for the vast number of Christ's adherents during His time on Earth, ensuring they would be better able to show those virtues in their own lives and thus undergo soul ascension when they passed away. The fact that they wrote down all of Christ's accomplishments and published a whole Bible for everyone to learn from further advanced the spread of virtue on Earth. On a spiritual level, the successful completion of Bestowal brought the entire planet closer to the Universal Father, in a way, sharing the advantage of Christ's Light-infused DNA with all of humanity. This made it even easier for human souls to ascend since they started closer to God.

Communion with God the Father established

Christ also enabled humans to more immediately and closely commune with God. Christ, Himself always had a particularly close relationship with God, but remember, He was, in a sense, a sort of emanation from God's essence Himself. Now, such a being undergoing Bestowal on a particular planet puts that planet closer to the Universal Father on its own, but even further than that, the intensity of the struggle Christ endured during this particular Bestowal changed the whole planet's spiritual alignment. The Universal Father now pays particular attention to Earth and its inhabitants. Now, many Earthlings, though not all of us, can reach God directly through prayer, with Him or at least His highest lieutenants providing us with even more guidance and protection.

Immediately after Christ's ascension to his rightful throne of the universe, Christ and God dispensed the "Spirit of Truth", which enabled faster spiritual growth among the human species. The Spirit is Truth is an increase in the conscious awareness that is bestowed for all of the earthlings and is anchored into the mother earth group consciousness. This has enabled an increase in light quotient for the entire planet. The Holy Spirit was and is always present; its communication circuits are in the basic fabric of the creation of the universe itself. Spirit of truth is different as noted above.

Anchoring of the great light

With the presence of the creator of the universe, Christ on Earth a great light has been anchored for all of Earth's existence. This has facilitated the opening of communication circuits that were previously closed when the earth was taken over by Lucifer/Satan. These communication circuits help earthlings to communicate with God's divine emissaries. Also, this has greatly tilted the War in favor of Light.

It is our duty to hold this light firmly and be its anchor until the savior comes again in the "Second coming" to annihilate and eradicate darkness for eternity.

WHAT IF CHRIST FAILED AND SATAN WON

Now that we understand what exactly transpired during Christ's temptation, and what the benefits of His victory were, it is time to examine what the true stakes of that great spiritual battle really were. In the final chapter, we are going to explore how Christ could have succumbed to Satan's temptations, and what would have happened if He had, thus demonstrating why we should be very, very grateful indeed that He instead succeeded and refused all of the tricks and traps of darkness.

This may seem blasphemous to most Christians or churchgoers. Rest assured, the intent of this chapter absolutely is not blasphemy, nor is it intended to impugn Christ. Far from it! Rather, this chapter will show why we should be so grateful to Christ, why His struggle and sacrifice were deeper than we might initially understand, and how He saved us from a very, very bad fate. This is the real turning point in earth's history. This event turned the favor of the tide to light.

The Importance of Preparation

There are a variety of ways in which errors or omissions in the study before Christ directly confronted Satan could have led to catastrophe. What if Christ didn't have his Father's presence inside him? Without God's direct divine assistance in fortifying Christ's spirit before Satan arrived, Christ might have been more susceptible to their taunts and tricks. They could have used their spiritual influence to overpower Christ's will and turn Him over to them. Now, God did leave Christ at the time of the temptation, for the reasons described in the previous chapter, but God's strength was still present in Christ even after the departure because they had spent so much time together beforehand. Without that, Satan might have succeeded.

What if Christ's human ego had overtaken His higher senses? This is a major reason many ordinary human beings often fall into Dark schemes. As important as our egos—the parts of our souls dedicated to the upkeep of our material body and our social relationship—may be, they must always play second fiddle to the higher spiritual aims that direct us after death. But the ego is a powerful thing. If Christ had let it overwhelm Him, as many people do, He would have been distracted by the offers of food and worldly power described in Satan's first two temptations and gone over to the Darkness because of them.

What if Christ thought all of the communications and visions he received from the Father and the angels were just fabrications of His ego? That would have been a danger on the opposite extreme, becoming too suspicious of the ego. While it can distract you from higher spiritual matters, it can never fake spiritual communication all on its own. If Christ had drawn that conclusion, He would have disregarded all the assistance and teaching God and the angels had been trying to give Him just before the confrontation, making Him much weaker and more vulnerable.

By the same token, what if Christ thought He had been going insane if He had visions or visitations? That would have been even worse. Christ would have thus been unable to even discern what was real and what was not in any case. This might have been an advantage to an extent when He was being tested by Satan; it is possible He would have said "these visions from the Devil are insane hallucinations as well" and ignored everything Satan said anyways. However, it would have rendered Him entirely unable to perform His duties as an emissary of Light later on, since He would have discarded Light visions as merely products of insanity. Thus, even if they would not subvert Him directly, Satan would have conquered Earth eventually anyway.

That would have been possible only if Christ did not really know Himself, His purpose, and His divine heritage. Thankfully, through his trenchant conversations with the Father from childhood onwards, Christ fully realized that He was not only a human being, even though He loved them, taught them, and had infinite compassion for them. If Christ did not have this knowledge, however, He would not have been as determined on a personal level to follow the will of the Universal Father from whom He emanated and thus would have been more likely to be entranced by Satan's offers.

Finally, and most horrifying of all, Christ could have possibly rejected the Father within himself. This would have been a completely radical repudiation, even worse than Lucifer's original rebellion, because Christ would have been rejecting His own nature consciously, not just making a mistake about whether He was sane or not, or being entranced by the pull of His own ego. It is almost impossible to tell what would have happened in this case: Perhaps Christ would have joined the Lucifer Rebellion to spite the Father, or perhaps He would have started His own rebellion. But in any case, He certainly would not have saved the world as well as the forces of Light as He did. There are several other flaws of individual personality which could have caused Christ to lose on Mount Hermon as well:

- **Not trusting His divine self:** Even if He had accepted all the visions He had seen and acknowledged His relationship with the Universal Father, it is possible Christ would still have lost faith in that divine aspect of Himself. That would likely have resulted in Him failing the final test; He would have attempted suicide in the hopes that angels would save Him because He would have lost faith in the divine plan. That would have shattered His relationship with God and likely allowed Satan to win Him over to their side, or at least derailed the progress of His Bestowal, perhaps forcing Him to repeat it.

- **Not trusting His inner journey:** If Christ had lost faith in all He had learned over the course of both His sojourn on Mount Hermon and His entire life up to that point, He would have lost the lessons that allowed Him to resist Satan's enticements. Thus, only firm belief in Himself, and confidence that He as a person had truly grown all on His own (rather than simply reflecting the strength of others), was

what saved Him from defeat in this
respect.

- **Not trusting His communion with the
  Father with-in:** Again, to the same extent
  and for the same reasons, if Christ had lost
  faith in His direct connection with God, it
  would have created an opportunity for
  Satan to manipulate His doubts and
  convince Him that God was not truly in
  control, leading Him to either Lucifer or
  His own rebellion.

- **Human ego becoming stronger than the
  divine self within:** Part of the reason for
  His isolation on Mount Hermon, as well as
  the many activities He undertook
  throughout His mortal life, was to gain
  control of His human ego and make sure it
  was entirely yoked to His higher divine
  self. This ensured that the natural human
  desires for material goods as well as fame
  and fortune never outweighed His
  spiritual goals in the ways He behaved and
  acted out in the world. Now, if Christ's ego
  had not been thoroughly tamed and
  disciplined by the time of His temptation,

89

the prospect of fame and power, or even (a worst-case scenario) mere food, would have been enough to make Him forget His divine purpose. He would have given in to immediate, short-term gratification and turned stones to bread—thus forcing Him to accept Satan's authority—or agreed to serve Satan in return for ruler-ship over the world, with a desire for fame outweighing a desire for good and service to others.

- **Insufficient preparation or not enough spiritual experiences before the temptation:** As described above, Christ painstakingly and exhaustively prepared for His confrontation with the dark lord. He prayed, spoke with God personally, meditated, got all His mundane necessities out of the way, strengthened Himself physically with exercise and good eating before fasting on Hermon, performed introspection and self-reflection, and so on. He also had many spiritual experiences; even though He did not perform miracles publicly, He still spoke with guardian angels who manifested to Him before leaving Him alone during His test. If He had not done all of this, He would have fallen to Darkness. Perhaps if He was too physically weak, His ego would have overwhelmed him. Perhaps He might have thought His visions and visitations from higher beings were hunger-induced hallucinations, and so on.

- **Too busy with mundane activities and being unable to focus on God or spiritual activities**: This was another reason Christ decided to spend so much time alone on Mount Hermon. Our relationships with our friends, the responsibilities we have at our jobs, and so on, are important parts of our human lives, surely. However, they must never be allowed to eclipse our divine destinies or our concern for spiritual matters. If Christ had spent too much time taking care of His family or working His mundane job as a carpenter, He wouldn't have been able to learn all the important lessons revealed by communion with God or strengthen His personal spirit and awareness of the battle between Light and Dark. Thus, when He faced Satan, He might have been little more than an ordinary carpenter and fallen into temptation as an ordinary carpenter would have.

- **If Christ was not born with "Divine DNA," He would have had a hard time just like normal human beings:** Additionally, Christ's physical constitution was special in many ways, just like His divine nature and mentality. Just as our DNA can make us more or less susceptible to certain diseases, certain strands of Light DNA make us more receptive to assistance from higher powers. As mentioned before, Christ's DNA represented the absolute apex of this. If He had been born in an ordinary person's body, even if He had all the training and self-discipline in the world, He would not have been able to commune with angelic beings as readily, and His constitution would not have been as inherently resistant to Dark energies. Thus, Satan might have been able to expend their spiritual energy to overcome Christ's physical body, bringing Him to his knees and forcing Him to submit, dooming mankind and planet Earth.

- **If spiritual ripening has not taken place, He would have given in to the temptation:** Finally, we must remember that all of the above considerations, ranging from communion with God, physical, mental, and spiritual preparation and conditioning, the triumph of will over ego, and so on, are all part of an interconnected whole. If even one of those aspects of Christ's personality had been lacking, He would have failed completely due to the reasons described above. This is why "spiritual ripening" was so important. Ripening refers to the process of coordinating one's development in all mental and physical spheres so that your advancement in one field lifts you up in another, and vice versa, so that your spirit as a holistic whole is advanced. If this process of spiritual ripening had not occurred, all of Christ's development in each individual attribute He possessed would not have led to Him being a stronger whole person: He would have been less than the sum of His parts rather than more, so to speak. And that flawed whole would have been much more susceptible to subversion, making Christ lose to the dark lord.

Why is this event so Critical? What are the Consequences of Failure

This event is very vital because it was the starting point of Jesus' victory over the devil, and this victory was extended to all humans and also to all of the universe by extension. This was the event that turned the tide in favor of light. Now that we know of the different ways in which Christ could have failed, what would the effects on the world and the entire universe have been if He had done so? Very dire, as it turns out. We would almost certainly not be here right now if any of those terrible scenarios had come to pass! Here is a description of what Satan would have done if Christ had not stopped Satan cold in his track:

History would have completely changed; even our calendar might not have looked like it is currently

Because of His victory over darkness, the calendar took a new turn, and we now number our days after the death of Jesus Christ. He was a turning point in history. His impact is felt not only by humans but all of creation and creatures. This might not have been the case if Christ gave in to Satan temptations.

Earth would have fallen to Darkness manifesto

If Christ had accepted Satan's temptation, they would then become the Dark Lords of the entire universe. Given Christ's power, He would probably have become Lucifer's second-in-command, as Lucifer would almost certainly not have been willing to give up lordship over his own rebellion

Darkness spreads across the Galaxy and to other parts of the universe

This would permit Darkness to spread exponentially far beyond Earth. All the various solar systems and nebulae in our galaxy would be vulnerable to Satan's domination. Light-aligned princes would be overthrown from other solar systems and galaxies, to be replaced by Satan's foul minions. Many higher beings, both more highly evolved beings on other planets as well as purely spiritual beings from higher realities, would almost certainly join the forces of Darkness. After all, human beings have a tendency to follow whoever seems the strongest, and the same applies to most creatures, both other planes of existence as well as angels and spirits (even though they may be more powerful and wiser than most mortals, they are not as strong of will as truly divine beings like the Creator of the Universe). By subverting the ruler of the entire universe, Satan would have seemed like he had the advantage, and that momentum was with his rebellion. Thus, many mortals and angels alike who had previously been skeptical of his cause would flock to join it under the misguided belief that they would profit in the end.

Many planets and life would have been destroyed

It is therefore possible that the Earth itself, along with many other parts of this galaxy at least, would have been completely destroyed. Remember, Satan cares for absolutely nothing and no one except himself and self-aggrandizement. He would have not the slightest concern with planet Earth's environment and biosphere. Under his evil control, the planet would be covered with factories and power plants spewing both physical and spiritual pollution. In addition to preying on the souls of its residents, Satan would likely have exploited every last bit of material resource (ores, chemicals, etc.) he could wrench from Earth no matter how much it damaged the world. After a few centuries of this, it is very likely the planet would collapse in on itself, or at least be reduced to completely lifeless rock. Satan would then do the same to other planets in the galaxy, exploiting both their residents and the physical resources of their world, until huge sections of the Milky Way were completely shorn of resources and left lifeless

Lucifer probably would have become the Chief of the Universe

Christ would still have become the Planetary Prince, however, Lucifer could have become the chief of the universe. This illustrates the Universal Father's steel-strong devotion to the freedom of His creations. God does not actively interfere in the actions and decisions of lower creatures because He absolutely respects our free will, even when we choose wrongly. Our lives would be meaningless (we would be nothing but puppets) if we could do nothing except what God willed, and, for that reason, He is willing to tolerate even the greatest rebellions like that of Lucifer, so that all of us can eventually choose righteousness of our own free will, not because we were forced to. Thus, even if Christ gave in to Satan's temptation,

God would still respect His decision, and still allow Him to assume lordship over planet Earth, as was already owed to Him. If this had actually happened, it is most likely Satan/Caligastia would have remained as the planetary prince of Earth.

Many higher beings probably converted over to Lucifer's plan

The Bible says 1/3 of Angels were deceived by Lucifer/Satan to join the rebellion against God. If Christ goes over to darkness, then the number of angels would probably be so much more. This will put the entire universe and heavenly realms in jeopardy.

There would be no disciples and no ministry

All that Jesus ever did was sponsored by the Spirit of the highest God that resides in him. Considering the ministry of Jesus, it is the one that gives us the pattern to do ministry the right way and to act as a leader in our given ministry. He taught us how to walk in the supernatural realm while doing the world of God right here on earth. Imagine there was no one to call Peter out of his uncertainty and give him a golden life; imagine there was no group of people who would sustain the revival that birthed the Holy Spirit. Imagine no one running a ministry that brings hope to the lost and love to the bitter; imagine no one went about doing good and calling the lost of Israel back home to their owner. It wouldn't be a nice experience for us who have once been referred to as gentiles.

Imagine the man at Bethsaida dying as a sick man instead of being healed, imagine the woman with the issue of blood dying after many attempts, imagine the wonderful revelations that made life easy not ever getting through to us because Apostle Paul might not have seen the light.

The new testament Bible probably would not exist

Finally, most obviously but also most significantly, the Bible would not exist in any form we would recognize. There would be no Sermon on the Mount, no mercy towards the adulterous woman, no healing of the sick, and no banishing of the demons for people to hear about. Not only that but the Old Testament would have been destroyed as well! Doing Satan's bidding, Christ would have directed His followers to destroy ancient Jewish wisdom rather than preserve it. Everything the Bible contains, all the inspiration it has brought to people the world over, would have been completely destroyed and could never be recovered.

Human communion with God would have been difficult

Communion with the Universal Father would have been difficult or lost. Due to Christ's Bestowal on Earth, the planet was given a special relationship with God, making it much easier for its inhabitants to commune with Him and gain wisdom from Him. If Christ joined the Dark, one of His first moves would have been to split Earth's astral and etheric spheres as far away from the heavenly ones as possible, making it nearly impossible for ordinary people to hear God's voice.

Not only Earth but the entire galaxy might have been under quarantine

We have seen that Earth had been under lock-down since Lucifer/Satan's takeover of planet Earth. All spiritual communication circuits have been shut down, thereby isolating Humanity from the rest of creation. This is the main reason for Humans to not know your space Angelic brothers and sisters. I discussed this more in my book "The Real Matrix series". I highly recommend it if you like to dive deep into the War in Heaven and the philosophies of dark and light forces. Darkness spreads like a virus, so it is quite possible that a bigger chunk of the universe could be locked-down or under quarantine.

Earth would continue to be a prison planet

In this way, Earth would be turned into a sort of prison planet. In addition to exploiting its resources, Satan/Lucifer would lock in all human beings and never permit us to leave. Not only would our souls be unable to ascend, but we would all be eternally trapped on Earth to serve as a power source for Darkness. Remember, just as ascending souls produce positive energy for the Light, souls trapped by Darkness within a single karmic cycle produce a lot of evil energy for the Darkness to exploit. In a situation similar to the famous Matrix movies, humanity will have been turned into nothing but living batteries to fuel the evil machinations of an alien enemy, completely prevented from living our own lives and reaching our full potential as individuals. A terrible fate indeed!

Access to higher levels of consciousness would be difficult

Ascension of souls to higher planes of existence would therefore become very difficult or almost impossible. Had Christ failed, this would have come to pass for several reasons. First, consider the perversion of karma mentioned above. Lucifer would rob most people of good karma regardless of how they lived, thus making it impossible for them to ascend. Second, with the most famous and powerful human, with a Divine nature as well, preaching evil rather than good, ordinary people on Earth would be misled and have no idea how to live the kind of moral life that would lead to ascension. Finally, under Satan's rule, the Earth would be full of all kinds of vampires, wraiths, and other Dark-aligned spirits that hurt people's minds and absorb their spiritual energy, thus keeping human souls trapped in Darkness and unable to ascend.

As the soul evolves, it is bestowed with intelligence, the use of reason, and thus the ability to perceive God's existence and follow His will. This process is continuing today, as human beings grow smarter and more civilized with every generation, hopefully leading to a peaceful and prosperous world in the future. This is also occurring on a spiritual level: Light DNA strands have been slowly worked into the human genome generation after generation, whether from favorable couplings between certain people or direct involvement from angels and higher beings. The intent of all this, as described above, would be to make humanity more aligned with God's teachings.

DNA manipulation to subvert the growth of the species

If Christ had given into temptation, this beautiful process would have been completely reversed. Satan would dictate who could pair with whom with an iron fist, trying to breed out light-aligned DNA just like the Nazis in the 20th century attempted. Satan would even try to out-rightly exterminate those people with Light DNA strands! Additionally, he would try to damage the human genome so that generation after generation of humans would be born dumber and weaker, making us less likely to throw off Satan's yoke and better as thralls to the Dark's schemes.

CONCLUSION

There are several lessons we can draw from everything examined here.

As mentioned above, we should all be grateful that Christ actually did resist Satan's temptations, and thus prevented all the nightmarish scenarios described in the previous sections from coming to pass. However, this should also remind us to treat every day of our own, mundane lives as if it were of cosmic significance. Yes, most of us may not directly confront the dark lords or even the lower-ranked dark beings directly. However, the fact that Christ found our world so important that He would descend upon it, and the fact that He endured such a difficult trial on Mount Hermon all to protect us, is proof that our struggles are very far from unimportant. Perhaps we will not be tempted by Satan himself, but we will always be subtly tempted by money, fame, power, or even basic necessities to forget the divinity we each have within us.

Christ's triumph in the wilderness and the knowledge of the Dark (literally) future that awaited us had He failed, serves as an example for us to emulate and a warning of what happens if we don't, even on smaller scales. For us as individuals, resisting temptation might not save the world on its own, but it certainly can save our individual souls and help us ascend to higher levels of existence after we pass on. And Christ wanted above all for us human beings to grow close to His Father just as He did. That would be the greatest way of commemorating His victory. So go forth, do good, and love God, just as Christ commanded!

By Christ's victory over Devil, Heaven's gates are open welcoming you are me into His eternal kingdom.

THANK YOU

I want to personally Thank you for reading this book.

I have poured my Heart and Soul into these pages. I hope you have gained some valuable insights from the information presented. Please consider leaving your valuable review. Your review and feedback are important to me. Thank you so much.

⭐ ⭐ ⭐ ⭐ ⭐

One Click Review:
https://www.amazon.com/review/create-review?&asin=B0BJRWPHCR
or Scan to write a review:

"What takes place on Earth is very important to Heaven." - Trinity Royal

In the previous chapters, you've learned about the spiritual forces at play throughout history and in the world right now. Even though they are unknown to the vast majority of humanity, you have chosen to open your eyes and discover how they have been and are influencing you and everyone around you. As Morpheus would say, You have taken the red pill.

Chapter: Clarion call from God to all the Angels in the Heaven

With the knowledge you now possess, it is time to move on to more advanced topics where you will gain significantly more depth of knowledge. While you've learned about the spiritual Matrix, and how Dark-aligned and Light-aligned entities influence Earth–whether by enslaving humans or liberating them, encouraging selfishness rather than altruism, and so on, now you'll see specific instances of these activities–and the rationales behind specific plans launched by both sides in the war– especially centering around Jesus Christ and His teachings.

Why God Needs Your Help

We have seen in the previous chapters that the War came to be centered on planet Earth. Earth is the epicenter of the battle between Dark and Light. What happens here affects the rest of the Universe.

Due to this, the human race has become God's prized possession, and our planet Earth– also called Urantia in higher realms of consciousness– is the site of many of God's most important plans and a storehouse of His most valuable resources. For the purposes of this book, we don't need to go too far into the details of the Universal Father's creative activity, or every one of His agents. Here, we will simply go over the broadest, most basic points of Earth's history you need to know to get a grasp of what you need to do to help the forces of Light.

God's own son "the Son of God" is Christ, who is also the creator of the Universe. Millions of years ago, Christ manipulated many nebulae to form stars, and thus our galaxy, and around one of these stars at the edge of one of these galaxies is the Milky Way. Each galaxy consists of numerous solar systems and planets.

When our Creator created this planet, He noted that there was something special about this little blue orb, it became known as the "seed" planet. The seed planets are considered special as new souls are developed on these kinds of planets. The seed planets are the training ground for young Souls on an evolutionary path. There are very few in number in this part of our galaxy. Christ with the help of Trinity consciousness (God the Universal Father, Eternal, Son, and Infinite Spirit) created the Human species. So we are created in His "likeness" as the scriptures state, making the residents of our planet particularly important for the plans of both God and Satan.

Human beings evolved empathy, compassion, altruism, and especially religious feelings much earlier in our development than was the case for sentient beings in other worlds. As a result, the spiritual energies produced by the development of human souls, whether ascending towards higher consciousness realms as the Light desires or chained down to this lower dimensional consciousness as the Dark desires, far outweigh those produced by even heavenly beings in the universe. Since the war has been at a stalemate in the rest of the Universe for a very long time, with neither Lucifer's forces nor the Light has been able to dislodge the other, Earth has taken center stage as the decisive point. Darkness, unfortunately, has managed to make significant in-roads on our planet and has advanced its plans very far. On the other hand, the Universal Father has plans of his own involving His most powerful agent here: Jesus Christ, whom we shall learn more about in future chapters. This should suffice as an overview of the Universal Father treasures humanity in particular so much.

Effects of the Rebellion

Now, due to Lucifer's rebellion, discussed in previous chapters, God has had a very difficult time reaching out to humanity, protecting and guiding us, despite how highly He valued us. The path for growth toward the Light was growing harder and harder for us, with many obstacles placed in our way. Here are some of the ways Darkness has interfered with us:

- **No real religious teachings**. There have been many great religions started by enlightened prophets which have been stamped out by the Dark. Humanity has been made to forget these religions and their teachings to delay the growth of many strong souls and prevent knowledge about the great spiritual conflict from spreading widely.

- **Manipulation of teachings**. Cunning agents of Darkness have manipulated some teachings of religions throughout history–and in the present day–to sow confusion and make it even harder for seekers to attain genuine knowledge of Heaven and higher spiritual realms.

- **Over-emphasis on the process:** Partially due to machinations from the Dark, but also due to honest mistakes which built up over time, much of humanity has become too focused on ritual–rather than finding their own individual "spark" of God within themselves.

Finally, whereas direct communication with God is possible on higher realms that are more vibrationally attuned to Paradise–the Veil or Matrix which envelopes Earth has cut us off from the Divine in some way. Only if we are very fortunate can some of us access higher realities, and often only in dreams; communion with the Universal Father Himself is very rare, with only the Bestowal of Christ giving us hope (described in the next chapter).

Even so, there are some agents of the Light who have come to Earth to assist us in reaching higher consciousness levels, even if they were not in direct contact with the Divine. Some gods in ancient polytheistic or henotheistic religions were heavenly messengers who came to help Humanity in the evolution process. Also religious figures like Lord Buddha or Lord Krishna, philosophers like Aristotle, Plato, Zeno of Elea, Confucius, and some modern-day personages like Martin Luther King. Some angels even gave inspiration to great inventors and teachers, like Jonas Salk–creator of the polio vaccine, Albert Einstein, and other Nobel Prize winners.

All these people were sent or influenced by the Light to guide mankind towards the climactic event which will occur soon, in the present time we are living in. The Dark has also influenced our world in many ways, both enslaving individual humans, trapping their souls, encouraging the evolution of dark cults, and, teaching other individuals selfish methods of increasing their power and influence. Some Dark agents manifested in this world directly, putting on human disguises, while others merely contacted ordinary people seeking power and subtly guided them into the shadows. Many Dark agents or servants settled as kings, queens, or great and bloody conquerors. Adolf Hitler and Ghenghis Khan are two such examples. Less famously, Dark agents generally tried–and are still trying–to infiltrate large, powerful, centralized governments to control information and how people lived, to ensure as few as possible could ascend.

They also manipulate the genetic code of humanity, to cut out strands of DNA carrying Light codes–such as nobler, more altruistic temperaments, higher attunement to spiritual realities, a higher propensity to dream–and so on. Despite both sides doing their best throughout hundreds of thousands of years, Light was never able to break Dark's grasp on the world, and Dark could never remove every trace of Light from Earth, even as its influence steadily grew. Thus, the war on Earth was grinding down into a stalemate as well; whatever advantages Dark had would take many, many centuries to come to fruition. Before that can happen, the forces of Light desire to strike a shattering blow against Satan/Lucifer. The fallen Morning Star, cunning as he is, anticipated that, and is attempting to gather his forces for his decisive annihilation of Light on Earth, which will allow him to capture the planet and turn all of the prodigious energy humans produce into his ends.

God's Counterattack

As the situation on Earth is rapidly heating up, the Universal Father focused more and more of His energies and attention on it. About 200,000 years ago, He made a clarion call to all of His angels to focus on humanity and do all they can to uplift the consciousness of this blue orb. God is no fool and made clear to His angelic forces that this would likely be the most difficult mission they had ever attempted ever in their entire existence. God also emphasized to them this struggle was worth it, for He realized how unique and powerful humanity is due to its peculiar evolutionary history, and thus He loves humanity and Earth more than any other place in the Universe. Much of God's focus is on humanity and earth at the present time. This is an absolute fact.

This clarion call rang out wide to all of Heavens and Paradise. The mission was simply to save Humans and Earth. A mission like this was never attempted in the history of creation.

Since this was unique, a vast number of angels had no idea what to expect and did not sign up for the mission. Given the incredible skills, the angels possessed, very many of them could not take it for fear of the unknown. Many were afraid of the struggle and Satan's forces in general and were also uncertain of the outcome. Most have already witnessed the devastation caused by Lucifer's rebellion in the Heavens. After all, such an endeavor had never been attempted before, and no histories existed in the great archives and annals of Heaven that could give any guidance on a war like this.

The angels who raised these concerns did not have full faith in the Universal Father's victory, so they chose to sit out the battle and wait and see who would win. Others did not want to limit their consciousness by focusing on one planet in one system in one planet of the vast Universe.

In fairness to these seemingly cowardly angels, fighting Satan's forces on Earth is a truly monumental task. The Matrix surrounding Earth has several characteristics that make things harder for the Light than the Dark.

However, some angels did have faith in God and Christ and said "yes" to this divine mission. There were at least 144,000 of these according to the Holy Bible. These are the angles who have agreed to come into the Matrix and be part of the Matrix, mingle with evolving Human souls, and increase the vibrations of Human consciousness thereby helping God and the cause of light. These angels were known as descended angels. According to a divinely orchestrated plan, these brave angelic souls planted themselves at predetermined strategic points of Human evolution to become teachers, preachers, inventors, gurus, sadhus, scientists..etc. Basically to teach and help evolve Humanity.

Then I looked, and behold, the Lamb was standing on Mount Zion, and with Him one hundred and forty-four thousand, having His name and the name of His Father written on their foreheads. – Revelations 14:1

However life is not all rosy for these brave angels; by being in the Matrix, all of them got caught up in the illusion of the Matrix, and most if not all forgot their divine origins and inter-mingled with humans over the period of 200,000 years. This has helped to manipulate the DNA of the Human species, thereby evolving the human species faster and closer to God. If Light wins, these brave angels will enjoy all the splendor and accolades they have earned.

The Matrix prevents spiritual beings from heavenly realms from passing into Earth. They are only allowed in if a resident of Earth, within the Matrix itself, specifically asks them to enter. This is called the doctrine of non-interference. Some beings can get around this, but it is extremely rare, and Dark forces like demons and shadow-whisperers more often do this. The great Bestowal of Christ was one exception to this rule in Light's favor. Another exception was the case of 'original seeders,' angels who visited humanity in distant past eons to place Light information in our genomes.

The effects of the Matrix on the development of the soul itself present another obstacle to the cause of Light due to loss of memory. Souls, ignorant as they are, cannot easily coordinate with each other, or angelic beings, and must rely on their internal abilities to evolve, which can be made easier if the bodies to which they are reincarnated possess useful strands of Light-aligned DNA. In this regard, humans possessing these types of DNA should mingle as much as possible with the rest of the human population to spread them far and wide and to future generations, but again, since accumulated knowledge is lost, this is harder to do. Souls must also learn their own lessons, rather than being taught, how to avoid the pitfalls of the Dark, transform Dark energies into Light ones, and enhance the collective consciousness of humanity.

Given all this, you can imagine why God is personally concerned with this war on a single small planet and refuses to give up on the human race. It is extremely important for Him and the Light to win this war, as so many of His strongest angels have already invested so much. In other words, not only are human souls at stake, but Paradise and other types of angels from higher heavenly realms also have vulnerable souls that might be at risk if they lose. Thus, God has a vested interest in you—yes, you! He wants your soul to grow, advance, and improve your spiritual life so you can help in the struggle. This will determine whether Light or Dark wins in the end.

If you like this preview...you will love this book. Get it today

Chapter: Various Levels of Heaven

The information included in the next two chapters is fairly advanced. It is a part of this book because it gives a complete picture of the different levels of Heaven as it relates to our location on the planet Earth.

It would only be natural if the previous chapters led to further questions about the ongoing development of the soul, the structure of Heaven and Earth, and what the other worlds outside of this one are made up of.

Depending on one's spiritual maturity, some concepts might be new. Please do not get too caught up in the difficulties and complexities of this chapter. If it feels like this is too advanced for you, feel free to skip it.

Heaven is a location, not a mind concept

Most of us have some concept of Heaven, even if it has been characteristically one formed by movies like *What Dreams May Come or The Lovely Bones,* or thinking it involves meeting as in the movie *Bruce Almighty.* Just as a movie requires a set direction and props, Heaven may just as well be similarly designed, but by one of the best designers, set directors, and make-up artists combined into One and by God Himself. It is created by "the One", the Father who brings all things into being.

The many levels of Heaven are as deliberately designed as any stage or movie set and include an intentional structure and order to creation that has existed since the dawn of time. Most certainly when we come to understand that our very soul, spirit, and identity are equally quite remarkable, then it comes as no surprise that Heaven too is just as real and astounding a place as the rest of all creation. In this chapter, we will explore the basic physical structure of Heaven and the various levels this Kingdom possesses.

While we can dream and imagine the white puffy clouds as being pillows that tuck us into our angel feather beds at night, and eternal sunshine exists as our backdrop as we float through in the expansive blue sky each day, it's actually not like that! Rather, Heaven is an actual location and not a mind concept. As taught by Jesus, he said, "I go to prepare a place for you" (*New International Version*, 1973, John 14:2).

This place, Heaven, as told by Jesus, is prepared and planned. This intentionality of Heaven can set us at ease. We tend to put God in a box and try to explain with our limited conscious understanding what things are all about when in reality, God determines all, and we are only human after all. Imagine and allow for the incredible graces of our Holy Father to plan and have a dwelling place for us and know this to be true. When we can do this, the concept of Heaven becomes easily understandable and grasped as a relatable place that is waiting for us.

The Father is loving and He has prepared for you a multitude of worlds on which you will continue to accumulate experience. It is simply impossible to gather all of the experiences of your soul's destiny in just one world, and only the initial one at that. When you have the path of the whole of creation laid down before you, with limitless experiences and boundless worlds, there are eternal structures you will see that will amaze you along your journey.

The Structure of Heaven

While you may be a beginner or have many years of growing and expanding your spiritual foundations on your relationship journey with God the Father, you may already know that Heaven is a place with multiple locations. We have established that it is not one single place but that the number of locations is varied and even infinite. For some, this may be common knowledge, whereas, for others, it may be a new concept. Regardless, bringing you the reader to this point of awareness and comprehension is key for this part of the book and for the remainder of the chapters as we will begin to traverse the physical structures of Heaven as well as our layers of consciousness to get there. Be sure to go slow and take time to explore, understand, and integrate the following concepts that support ideas relating to the structure of Heaven, especially if some of these ideas may be new to you.

We can classify the structure of reality and worlds as categorized as layers into 3 broad categories that range from the material world being the most-dense to non-material as the least dense. Then there is Paradise where God, the deity resides.

1. Material worlds (physical worlds like Earth)
2. Semi-Material worlds (transition worlds, also called Soul or Morontia worlds)
3. Non-material worlds (Spirit Worlds)
4. Paradise (God's abode, beyond time and space)

The structure, makeup, and complexity of worlds increase as one moves from the lower to the higher dimensional levels not in physical complexity, but in their frequency. Imagine that each level corresponds with a dimension. The less-dense we are in the material world, the higher the frequency in the less-dense dimension. And, the frequencies of higher dimensions are more complex than the ones below. Let me explain this further. If we were to place living beings in the most-dense material plane, it is easy to comprehend that the chemical composition and complexity of the level above is higher than the level below yet appears and is more physically dense. Higher levels or dimensions require less food or sustenance than a lower-level living being would consume but are more complex in frequency. Overall, it is therefore safe to assume that food or sustenance requirements will reduce as body-form frequencies increase.

Think of it in relation to the concept of vapor that rises without having form or density. The higher you go, the higher the senses become and less sustenance is required. At some point, experiences beyond the five senses will start to open. This can lead to the understanding that the abilities that people have in the higher Heavens are more complex than what we are accustomed to and may be represented through advanced telepathy or having other super-sensory skills or powers that equate with being generally common for that level or dimension. Forget the internet, imagine how fast messages could arrive if they were simply sent and received on a mental signal that didn't require opening up your email and reading it, let alone finding the "on" switch. The three worlds are broken down individually and outlined below and will clarify the different levels of existence to which our human body, soul, and spirit can experience after our earthly death sleep.

The Three Worlds of Space and Time

Material world (Physical worlds like Earth)

The material world is right outside your doorstep. We are fully aware of this earthly plane that can be felt by the ground that we walk upon, the seasons that change in our geographical locations, and the tides of the water that rise and fall with each phase of the moon. Each part of our Earth and its sphere is made up of certain chemical elements, for example, periodic table elements that all have certain vibrational frequencies that are not only found within our bodies but also the planet as a whole. For those who are familiar with the Shuman resonance, it acknowledges that "each lightning burst creates electromagnetic waves that begin to circle around Earth, captured between Earth's surface and a boundary about 60 miles up. Some of the waves—if they have just the right wavelength—combine, increasing in strength, to create a repeating atmospheric heartbeat known as Schumann resonance" (Wilson, 2013). These incredible electromagnetic waves are present around us and keep us in the earth's container, grounded in physicality and energetic impulses that make up and define the material world. The Earth, as we know it, also contains physical and dense beings—we humans—that require food and sustenance for our bodies. It is the food that we consume that fuels our own living energy and keeps our cellular structure, blood flow, and heartbeat alive, all maintained within the unique properties of this material dimension.

Semi-material worlds (Transition worlds also called soul or Morontial worlds)

While Earth is a planet with a density we are certainly familiar with where we can walk, drive, and even fly in an airplane as part of our experience, what are the semi-material or transition worlds? *Morontia* is a term that refers to the vast level suspended between the material and the non-material (spiritual planes). There are many sub-levels within this realm. Each *Morontia* world is characteristically more refined, complex, and considerably less dense than the one below it.

While knowledge or even awareness of these worlds is not very common or well-known to most people, they are documented in the Bible.
One of Jesus' own disciples wrote about an 'enduring substance' of Heaven that can lead one to contemplate the existence of the *morontial* worlds, as it is written in Hebrews; "For ye had

compassion of me in my bonds, and took joyfully the spoiling of your goods, knowing in yourselves that ye have in heaven a better and an enduring substance." (*King James Bible*, 2017/1769, Hebrews 10:34). As you rise in these semi-material worlds, they become less dense and, according to this biblical reference, existence has a more timeless frequency that may be best measured and described as immortality. Once we begin to transcend the earthly realm, vibrational frequencies increase, and the spaces contain beings who are less dense and whose bodies need less food and sustenance for survival.

While it may be strange to think of beings other than humans who live in other dimensions and these angelic or other beings of reference are new to you, these beings living here have a body form technically called *Soul Body*. When Christ was resurrected, Christ's body was a *Soul Body* form. This is semi-material. If it was not, doubting Thomas would not have been able to touch the wounds of Jesus Christ whose biblical story demonstrates the importance of believing and having faith; "then he said to Thomas, 'Put your finger here, and see my hands; and put out your hand, and place it in my side. Do not disbelieve but believe.' Thomas answered him, 'My Lord and my God!' Jesus said to him, 'Have you believed because you have seen me? Blessed are those who have not seen and yet have believed'" (*New International Version*, 1973,). Not only does this story represent the power of faith during the time of Jesus' resurrection, but the form of Jesus' body was a *Soul Body*. If His body was fully spirit, He would not have a form to be recognized by the apostles during His resurrection. Many did not recognize Him at first glance, unless He revealed Himself, meaning He did not have a pure physical body. When we begin to imagine the spaces beyond our physical and material world, and the impermanence of our life and our own physical body, it clarifies how incredible our own human body is and the fact that a *Soul Body* and other creatures exist is entirely fathomable. Perhaps it is when we acknowledge the spiritual world and complete transcendence that many begin to scratch their heads and wonder if spiritual ascension is feasible. This semi-material world may introduce some notions of *Soul Body* and impermanence, but it is the spirit worlds that take us to yet a higher frequency even more astounding.

Non-material Worlds (Spirit worlds)

The spirit worlds might be easier to imagine if you have spent time watching science fiction movies of mythical realms and creatures that walk on other planets. While you witness and experience the visuals of these places through colorfully filmed productions, the spiritual world, distinct from the physical world, can be perceived just as incredible. But true depictions of the spiritual world may not be entirely possible due to subjective realities and our lack of ability to perceive them. I will do my best here to describe these spaces of the spiritual world that may not elude all of us.

According to the best of my knowledge and experience, there are numerous spirit worlds. As we can best imagine they are different from the material world grounded in the earth. The spirit worlds have energy wavelengths and celestial bodies that require food and substance yet at a much lesser frequency.

The spirit is 100% light and therefore there is no substance to the body form. There is no need for food or sustenance for the celestial beings that are 100% light because the spirit is self-generating. It is possible that many beings who are from spirit worlds came to Earth as planetary teachers and are walking among us.

If you can imagine the spirit as light, then it is possible to comprehend that the vibrations of a spirit being is very high, meaning that their frequency operates not on the dense emotions of fear, hate, or sorrow as an example, but contains more love, joy, and gratitude.

Aside from the amount of information that we can find on the internet these days, presently and historically we have seen pictures of these celestial beings with halos around their heads, like those of Christ, and maybe even floating above in the air. I believe this represents a self-generating glow of Spirit.

This representation of divinity or beings of divine stature is celestial beings who live in the spirit worlds that surround us and exist on different dimensions. The spirit world is a level that is one dimension lower than Paradise, the abode of the Holy God, the deity.

Paradise – God's abode

The best possible attempt to describe and define God's abode and utilize the most appropriate English word possible would be *Paradise*. This place isn't referring to the five-star hotel situated on the turquoise oceanfront property of a tropical island that we may dream about but, if you set your imagination on a place that is uniquely unfathomable to our limited consciousness, you might just be able to comprehend it.

Why is the word "Paradise" appropriate to refer to Heaven? When understanding the origin of the word Paradise from early English, French, and Latin, it has interestingly enough been directly translated as 'The Garden of Eden' (Etymonline, 2022). This makes this choice of the word quite appropriate, it appears, as it relates to the book of Genesis as one of the first Books in the Bible.

The Garden of Eden "is the story of the heavens and the Earth when they were made, in the day the Lord God made the Earth and the heavens" *(New International Version*, 1973, Genesis 2:4-6).

Paradise is used frequently throughout the Bible including in the book of Luke when it says, "and Jesus said unto him. Verily I say unto thee, Today shalt thou be with me in paradise" *(New International Version*, 1973,). Paradise is the dwelling place of the Trinity—God the Father, God the Eternal Son, and God the Infinite Spirit—and conjures many ideal qualities to define the Heavenly Kingdom.

Paradise is the indwelling place of all beings and is where God himself resides in the Kingdom of all eternity. When a person dies, the soul and, as we addressed in earlier chapters, the spirit detaches and goes to Paradise to be in the presence of God. If we can suspend the limitations of our human consciousness momentarily, we may be able to grasp the infinite concept of this resurrected place referred to as Paradise.

We can identify it as a place that has no time and exists in one eternal moment. Since everything created has movement, for example, the planets, stars, sun, and galaxies that are in constant motion and so in tune with the expansiveness of the universe and unequivocal harmony, there is another end of the spectrum.

It is possible to imagine that no time or space can exist either. Can you imagine it? Can you resonate with both perspectives of the duality of the existence within our universe created by God? Is it possible to comprehend or exist in absolute movement and utter stillness while being in a timeless place where God exists in all realms with an eternal presence? Many do believe this is possible.

I have created the image below representing the three worlds of time and space. Material worlds have physical body forms.

Semi-material heavenly worlds have Semi-material body forms also known as Soul body forms. The spirit resides in spirit worlds. Then there is Paradise which is beyond the time-space continuum.

There is a graduation process that happens as we progress in our evolution. We will talk about the graduation process between different forms shortly.

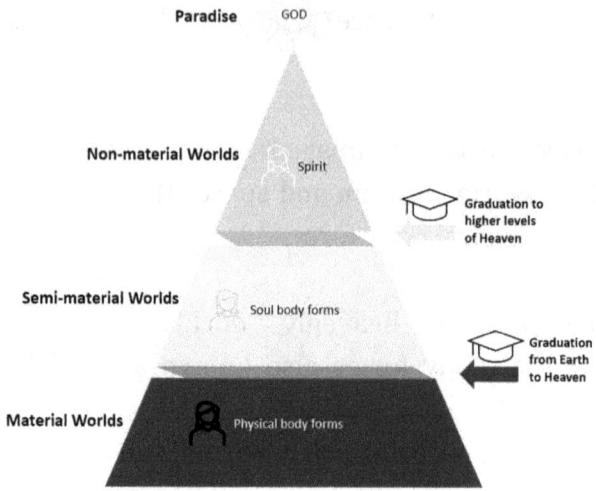

Paradise   GOD

Non-material Worlds   Spirit

Graduation to
higher levels
of Heaven

Semi-material Worlds   Soul body forms

Graduation
from Earth
to Heaven

Material Worlds   Physical body forms

WELCOME TO HEAVEN. YOUR GRADUATION FROM KINDERGARTEN EARTH TO HEAVEN

Scan Me

"I go and prepare a place for you, I will come back and take you to be with me that you also may be where I am." - John 14:3

Ever wonder **if Heaven is real**? What **proof** do we have?

How does one **go to Heaven**? What are the **minimum requirements for Heaven**?

Why *Life of Earth is your Kindergarten school*?

Trinity explores the following:

- *Isn't Heaven **just a mind concept**? What is the proof of its existence? Why do I even bother about Heaven? What is in it for me?*

137

- *What are the **minimum requirements to go to Heaven or the ticket booth to Heaven**?*
- *Why is life on Earth your **kindergarten school**?*
- *Are there **different levels to heaven? If so, how many? What are they? Does the time and space continuum exist in Heaven?** If so how different is it compared to Earth's time and space?*

"No eye has seen, no ear has heard, and no mind has imagined what God has prepared for those who love him." – 1 Corinthians 2:9

Ever wonder what your **life in Heaven will look like after your mortal death**?

Is there **Marriage** in Heaven? Do you have a **Family in Heaven**?

Do you have your **Parents or kids or your siblings** in Heaven?

Do you have **Sexual intercourse** in Heaven?

And what do you do all day? Is there a **daily Job**? Oh. And will you meet your **deceased family members**, friends, and relatives?

These are questions that curious minds like me ask. You will find **authoritative un-speculated** answers here.

Scan Me

Multiple Award-winning Book

"extraordinary book" "Definitely a five-star read" - [International Review of Books]

Ever wonder **why there is a War between GOD and the Devil?** Ever wonder how the **War in Heaven started or what the Lucifer Rebellion is**?

Ever wonder why War in heaven came to Earth or why darkness still exists on Earth? And why did God send Christ to Earth?

This book explores:

- How and Why did the **war in Heaven start**? How did the War in Heaven come to Earth?
- Why did **God send Christ** to planet Earth? Was it to save Humanity and the Universe?
- What exactly happened during **Christ's First Coming** event? What is expected during the Second Coming event?

Trinity takes us on a **journey beyond time and space** to find the answers to these questions that every believer should know.

Ever wonder why **there is a War between GOD and Devil?**

Ever wonder how the **War in Heaven started or what Lucifer Rebellion is?** **and why War in Heaven came to Earth** and why darkness still exists on Earth?

This book explores:

- How and Why did the **war in Heaven start?**
- How did the War in Heaven come to Earth?
- Why did **God send Christ** to planet Earth? Was it to save Humanity and the Universe?
- What are the effects of War on Earth and in Heaven?

- What exactly happened during **Christ's First Coming** event?
- What is expected during the Second Coming event?

I invite you to join me on a journey beyond space and time when the Lucifer Rebellion started and the reasons for Christ's First and Second Coming events.

*"The reason the Son of God appeared was to
destroy the Devil's work." – 1 John 3:8*

Is there an **UNSEEN world of Darkness** hidden
in front of our eyes?

Ever wonder why **Evil** exists on Earth?

Ever wonder how **Satan got to planet Earth a**nd
what exactly is the Dark Empire Agenda?

Ever wonder why Christ chose planet Earth for
His great Bestowal?

What is the **agenda of Darkness**?

Why do God and Christ let dark forces flourish on
Earth?

Does God have a plan? What is it?

What are the differences between **Demons, Evil Spirits, and Ghosts**?

How does **Selling one's Soul to the devil** happen?

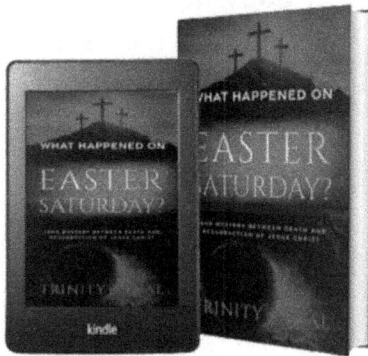

Scan Me

"A five-star read, absolutely."

" It stands to reason that Saturday was a critical time for Him"

"I highly recommend this incredible book as it takes the reader through both the physical and spiritual journey of Him as he underwent His transformation. *A five-star read, absolutely.*"

"I for one never really thought about that Saturday, so for me **it was a riveting experience**, learning about that previously overlooked time."

Ever wonder **what happened when Christ was inside the Tomb for 36 hrs** between death and resurrection?

Ever wonder **what body did Christ have after Resurrection?** and why the **resurrection process take 3 days?** why not 1-day or 2-days?

SOS - SAVE yOUR SOUL. WHAT HAPPENS AFTER YOU DIE?

Scan Me

"For what shall it profit a man, if he shall gain the whole world, and lose his own soul?" - Mark 8:36

Ever Wonder **What Happens After You Die**? Is it the end?

What did **Christ** Say about death and life after mortal death?

Is there a way to Save yOur Soul? If so How?

What exactly is **Soul** and **Spirit**, is it just a new age concept? What did Christ Say?

Trinity considered to be one of the bridges between Heaven and Earth, shares general Angelic knowledge. This book explores:

What are the unseen parts of us that make us who we are? What is left behind after Mortal death and what happens to these **unseen parts of us**?

What exactly is **Soul** and **Spirit**, is it just a new age concept? What did Christ Say?

Is there a way to Save yOur Soul? If so How?

Does Heaven actually exist?

Can a ticket to Heaven be guaranteed?

Scan Me

"I highly recommend this for anyone **who has ever suffered in their lives**, and, in all honesty, who hasn't?"

Why do **bad things happen to good people**?

Why does your **Life journey lead you to suffer?**

The Answer is to Heal You.

Your suffering is the epitome of a **blessing in disguise.** Wrapped in darkness and suffering, it removes the ground from beneath your feet and leaves you fearful, fragile, and devoid of meaning in life.

Most beings that we adore or worship have gone through dark times in their life. This includes Christ, Buddha, Gandhi, Nelson Mandela, Oprah, Abraham Lincoln, etc. This process is necessary as it redefines a person, re-makes one character, and chips away the darkness to bring out the luster of your **Real Self.** This is your **METAMORPHOSIS**.

Award-Winning Book

Our wounds are often the openings into the best and the most beautiful parts of us." -David Richo

Ever wonder **why suffering happens for no known reason...**

Ever wonder **why your Soul is longing...**

Have you ever felt like you have a **splinter in your mind, that does not let you off the hook..**

If so, **you are chosen for a purpose. There is GOD's hand working in your life.**

153

While there are many reasons people suffer (most are self-made or bad decisions or external in nature); the type of Suffering referred to as the "Dark Night of the Soul" has a clear and definite purpose. *The purpose is your Soul's growth.*

Your Answers and Healing await. Click on Buy Now.

War in Heaven came to Earth. Satan Rebellion:

https://dl.bookfunnel.com/ea12ys3dmk

Your Life in Heaven:

https://dl.bookfunnel.com/vg451qpuzs

REFERENCES

English Standard Version Bible. (2001). ESV Online.

Cairnes, Julie Von Nonveiller. (2019, September 15). The Battle between Light and Dark. https://medium. com/spiritual-warfare-the-new-predator/the-battle-between-light- and-dark-7bbccbeba738 –

Medium, Spiritual Warfare & The New Predator.

Candace Letters - https://Abundanthope.net

The Jesusonian Foundation. (2022, May 4). The Urantia Book. Truth-Book Quotes reference – Matrix movie series

Trinity is a multi-award-winning author and a spiritual warrior. While life might not always work out according to plan, Trinity was able to take valuable lessons from each new experience. Trinity grew and developed and now shares a passion for enlightening others on spiritual knowledge in the hopes of closing the gap between Heaven and Earth. Trinity's writings reflect the depths of a passion and desire to connect with everyone seeking spiritual growth and education.

You can learn more at

www.RocketshipPath2God.com or @

https://www.facebook.com/TrinityRoyalBooks